THE KNITTER'S

BOOK

OF

SOCKS

Cover and interior design by Jenny Kraemer
Front cover photography by Alexandra Grablewski
Illustrations by Kate McKeon

Published in the United States by Potter Craft, an imprint of the Crown Publishing Group,
a division of Random House, Inc., New York
www.crownpublishing.com
www.pottercraft.com

POTTER CRAFT and colophon is a registered trademark of Random House, Inc.

Library of Congress Cataloging-in-Publication Data

Parkes, Clara.
  The knitter's book of socks : the yarn lover's ultimate guide to creating socks that fit
well, feel great, and last a lifetime / Clara Parkes.
    p. cm.
  ISBN-13: 978-0-307-58680-3 (hardback)
  ISBN-10: 0-307-58680-4 ()
  1. Knitting—Patterns. 2. Socks. I. Title.
  TT825.P363 2011
  746.43'2--dc22
                              2011002682

Printed in China

10 9 8 7 6 5 4 3 2 1
First Edition

THE KNITTER'S
BOOK OF SOCKS

*The Yarn Lover's Ultimate Guide to Creating Socks
That Fit Well, Feel Great, and Last a Lifetime*

CLARA PARKES

POTTER
CRAFT
New York

CONTENTS

Introduction

Socks are the breakfast of our knitting diet, a physical and metaphorical underpinning to our day. They get us off to a good start, send us out into the world, and give a good indication of how the day will go. Is the cuff too tight? Frustration and discomfort from the get-go. Fabric won't breathe? A stifled day. Has the foot sprouted a hole? Or two? A sense of sloppiness prevails—along with a fear that you'll have to remove your shoes and expose your secret to the world.

But when fiber, twist, ply, stitch, and foot unite in a wholesome, well-balanced nutritious breakfast, the day is yours. You are proud, comfortable, confident. "Why, yes," you quickly answer, hoisting up your pant leg and slipping off your shoe for a better view, "I *did* knit them myself. Aren't they fabulous?"

I want you to feel this triumphant every day, which is why I've created this book about the art, science, and sheer pleasure of knitting socks from the yarn up. Many excellent sock-knitting books already exist, each offering gorgeous design ideas and ingenious techniques. But none of those books approaches socks exclusively from a *yarn* perspective. Without that information, a vital part of the sock equation remains a giant question mark.

Sure, you can knit socks out of just about anything, from dental floss to bailing twine and even licorice, just as you can make a stunning teakettle out of papier-mâché. As long as you never actually tried to use these items for their intended purposes, they'd be beautiful. But once we add functionality to the equation, our choices narrow.

Having ruled out bailing twine, the next logical step is to use a yarn that looks pretty and feels nice. But there's still much more to it.

If you've knit socks for any length of time, you may have already encountered one or two sock failures. Sometimes the pattern was to blame, sometimes the knitter. But more often than not, the problem was with the yarn—not elastic enough for certain stitches, too splitty for the needles you chose, or perhaps it blew a hole after just a few wearings. All easily avoidable, and you'll learn how.

I should note that so-called "sock" yarns can be used for all sorts of other projects, too, everything from shawls and blankets to sweaters and baby clothes. But this book focuses literally and exclusively on sock yarns as they are used for socks. It picks up where *The Knitter's Book of Yarn* left off, taking you deep into the complex and challenging structural universe of socks.

No other knitted garment experiences wearability demands as arduous as the humble sock. Hats and sweaters, shawls and scarves have it easy. Only socks must defy gravity and stay upright on our legs, cling to our calves without cutting off our circulation, hold tight to a foot that's jammed into an increasingly hot, humid shoe—and then endure being trampled on for countless hours while still remaining pretty to the eye. The well-conceived, well-constructed, handknitted sock will survive this endurance challenge with flying colors. It is a work of beauty.

HOW TO USE THIS BOOK

This book follows the sock-yarn life cycle from its early days as a pile of fluff to its final moments on a proud foot. We'll look at how common fibers may meet the demands of a sock, how a yarn's construction can further meet those demands, and how you can manipulate your stitches to coax even the most reluctant sock yarn into submission. You'll learn how to pair fiber, twist, ply, pattern, and even *stitch* for a happy sock, and how to modify sock patterns when necessary to better accommodate a specific yarn. By the end of this book, you'll be reading labels and squeezing skeins to get a better idea of what sock yarns can do—and you'll know how to compensate for what they can't. I want you to love every pair of socks you knit, and this book will help you do just that.

As always, I believe we learn best by doing, which is why I asked some of my favorite sock mentors to pitch in. Together, we've created twenty sock patterns that explore themes of fiber, durability,

and wearability from different stylistic angles that include lace, ribbing, cables, and colorwork. Even the designers were often surprised by what they discovered and ultimately created when conceiving socks from the yarn up.

Once you've grown familiar with all the necessary components of a successful sock, you'll be able to play with them, like interchangeable building blocks, confidently making adjustments in fiber, yarn, and stitch to concoct the ideal socks for your needs.

Of course, you could also launch right into the patterns—the knitter's version of salting your food before tasting it. In life and in knitting, any experience is broadened by knowledge. My hope is that you'll spend a little time up front reading more about the *why* and *how* of what you're doing before you cast on. I'd like you to understand what makes these socks work, and how you can put together your own nutritious breakfast from now on.

What a Sock Needs

Elasticity, strength, and absorption. Those three qualities dictate everything. An unhappy sock's demise can almost always be traced back to a deficiency in one of these areas, while a happy sock always has a healthy dose of all three qualities. Elasticity, strength, and absorption dictate both the knitting and wearing experience equally. Remember them, because they are the foundation of everything we'll explore in this book.

Lasting Elasticity

Hats have the luxury of resting on our heads, and sweaters enjoy the support of our shoulders and arms. Shawls can drape on our shoulders, and even knitted skirts have a natural shelf created by our waists. But socks must perform gravity-defying miracles. Starting at our toes, they enclose our foot, make a sharp turn at the heel, and then work their way up our leg. Just when things are starting to get good, we ask our socks to stop and sit there in midair, with no natural support whatsoever. Some kneesocks benefit from a natural shelf at the top of the calf, but the majority of socks have nothing.

The natural instinct would be to create as tight a material as possible to keep the sock from falling down. But the cuff encircles a calf that, by its very nature, does not like

IN THE STRETCH: FIBER COMPARISON

In an ideal world, we'd be able to stretch a yarn, let go, and have it return to its exact original length. But not all fibers snap back into shape with equal skill. Cotton, for example, is notoriously unfriendly in this regard. If stretched by 2 percent, cotton will only return to within 74 percent of its original length; wool will recover 99 percent of its original length. Meanwhile, nylon can be stretched by not 2, not even 4, but 8 percent and return to 100 percent of its original length. And Lycra? Tug it to 500 percent of its original length and it'll snap right back into place. Pure elasticity.

The ideal sock needs elasticity in order to stretch, stay up, and remain comfortable.

to be constricted. The fabric must therefore be flexible enough to hold snug without cutting off circulation. Making matters more challenging, the fabric also has to stretch up to twice its circumference to accommodate our heel every time we put on or take off the sock.

What we need is "elasticity," or the ability for a fiber to return to its original length after being stretched. This is the first cardinal requirement of all socks. You can have an elastic fiber, an elastic spin, or an elastic stitch—but you must have elasticity in there somewhere. Elasticity helps the sock embrace your leg without being too tight. It helps the cuff expand and contract every time you slip your heel through it. And it helps the sock stretch and flex with your foot as you move about your daily life. We love elasticity.

YOUNG'S MODULUS

How a fiber responds to all this tugging is often expressed visually in a curve, with stress shown along one axis (i.e., how hard you're pulling the fiber) and strain shown along the other axis (i.e., what happens to the fiber as you pull it). The curve ends when the fiber snaps. From a scientific perspective, the stress-strain curve demonstrates a fiber's "modulus of elasticity." The most famous such modulus is called Young's Modulus, after nineteenth-century British scientist Thomas Young. Things happen to fibers as you stretch them, and the goal of Young's Modulus is to show how much stress it took to make those things happen. Young's Modulus is expressed in the United States in pounds of force applied per square inch of fiber.

You may think that this level of scientific analysis couldn't possibly matter to a knitter, and for most purposes you may be right. Young's Modulus certainly isn't something you'll see listed on a yarn label. It's more crucial for the material in cables holding up a bridge or for the ropes holding up a rock climber—but it does help explain some of the mysteries we encounter in yarn. That's because a yarn that blends two fibers whose stress-strain ratios are dramatically different will be *weaker* than either fiber is individually.

How can that be? Simple: The fiber with the higher Young's Modulus is bearing a greater load of stress before the other fiber, which may actually be stronger, starts to carry its share. And when that other, possibly stronger fiber kicks in, the original fiber will have likely distorted, deformed, or snapped. A smart yarn manufacturer will modify the blend percentages accordingly. But not all do.

Brute Strength

A nice elastic sock is just the beginning. Once we've stretched the cuff beyond recognition, slipped our foot inside, and let the fabric return snugly back into place, we then do the unthinkable: We jam this beautiful knitted creation into a shoe and start walking on it.

To survive this kind of brutal treatment, a sock yarn needs to be strong. Ideally, the sock's strength comes from the fibers themselves, but it can be enhanced by the yarn's twist, ply structure, and even the stitches you form with it on your needles.

Socks need the kind of strength that can withstand the slow back-and-forth abrasion of everyday wear—but they also benefit from a little muscle power too.

ABRASION

When I say *strength*, I'm not necessarily talking about the kind that'll pull a pickup truck. I'm talking about the strength to withstand the small, slow, and persistent rubbing and chafing that gradually erode even the strongest of materials. Such wear is called *abrasion*, and a healthy sock needs to be made of both fibers and yarn that can resist abrasion, aided, if necessary, by abrasion-resistant stitches and knitting techniques (all of which we'll talk about in more detail later). The commercial hosiery world has special machines that test a fabric's abrasion and pilling resistance, the most famous of which is called the Martindale Abrasion Tester. For most knitters, however, our fabric-testing equipment consists of our foot, our shoe, and the unsuspecting finished sock. Which is why it's important to know as much about the yarn as possible before ever casting on.

TENSILE STRENGTH

Socks also benefit from a little of that truck-pulling strength as well. That's called *tensile strength*, or a yarn's ability to absorb energy without breaking. The higher the tensile strength, the more tension the fiber can resist before snapping. We tend to talk most about tensile strength in terms of groups of fibers, since that's how they exist in yarn. The breaking strength of individual fibers, on the other hand, is expressed in terms of their *tenacity*. Interestingly enough, two fibers with the same tenacity may have very different tensile strengths. Just like people, fibers can behave differently in groups than when they're alone.

To put tensile strength in perspective, nylon can absorb around 65,000 pounds (29,500kg) of force per square inch (6.5cm²) before breaking; cotton will absorb anywhere from 40,000 to 120,000 pounds (18,150–54,500kg)

per square inch (6.5cm²); and the humble wool fiber can withstand only an average of 17,000 to 29,000 pounds (7,700–13,150kg) per square inch (6.5cm²) before breaking. And yet wool remains the best fiber for socks. Why is this? Because of the third piece of our puzzle: the fiber's ability to deal with moisture.

Moisture Management

If we walked around in our stocking feet all day long, moisture management probably wouldn't matter as much. But most of us have to slip our sock-clad feet into shoes at some point during the day. They may be open-heeled mules, loose clogs, Crocs, flats, dress shoes, sandals, running shoes, you name it—but the point is, the sock must spend its day jammed inside a shoe, constantly buffering an increasingly warm, perspiring foot and a rigid shoe surface. For socks to

> *Just like people,*
> *fibers can behave*
> *differently*
> *in groups than when*
> *they're alone.*

HOW MOISTURE AFFECTS STRENGTH

Be aware that the more readily a fiber absorbs moisture, the more likely it is to weaken when wet—the only exception being cotton. This trait tends to be more of a concern with loose fabrics. A tightly spun, multiple-plied wool sock yarn knit at a very tight gauge, as is done with socks, should withstand water-induced vulnerability quite well. The only time I'd be remotely concerned is if you routinely wore your handknit wool socks on weeklong hiking expeditions through wetlands. But even then, I suspect you'd be fine—and happy.

do their job properly, they must be able to manage this heat and moisture in such a way that our feet maintain a steady, comfortable temperature without ever feeling too hot, damp, or clammy.

REGAIN

Here we meet one of my favorite words in the sock-yarn lexicon: *regain*. This refers to the moisture-absorbing properties of a fiber, expressed as a percentage of moisture present versus what would be present in that same fiber if it were oven-dry. Obviously, this number will constantly fluctuate, depending on the place and day. But, generally speaking, we want to seek fibers that have the highest possible regain. Especially in warm climates, the more moisture a sock can absorb, the less remains directly against our skin. Despite its stellar strength and elasticity, nylon averages only 1–4 percent regain. Cotton, on the other hand, has an average regain of 8.5 percent. That number sounds impressive until you notice that wool's average moisture regain ranges from 13 to 17 percent—and it can absorb up to 30 percent of its weight in moisture before ever feeling wet to the touch. This is why wool, despite that lower tensile strength, is such an optimal fiber for socks.

WICKING

There's another moisture-related term that can confuse things: *wicking*. It's the polar opposite of absorption. Instead of a fiber absorbing moisture and keeping it right there in place, wicking involves the migration of moisture *away* from an area of dense humidity and toward an area of less-dense humidity. For socks, the moisture would naturally migrate away from your skin and end up on the outer edge of the fabric.

Wicking relies on a capillary action found in synthetic fibers, primarily polyester, polypropylene, and microfiber (a superfine fiber that is less than 1 denier thick and

The ideal sock yarn has fibers that can manage heat and moisture to keep our feet comfortable and dry all day long.

usually composed of polyester). Often these fibers are also treated with a water-repellant coating to enhance their wicking capabilities.

Few of these specially treated fibers have found their way into handknitting yarns just yet—but they may soon. Just be aware that even these miracle fibers will cease to wick when all the fibers reach the same level of moisture.

A Willingness to Be Worked and Worn

Happy socks have an unspoken fourth element, too—a simple and obvious one. The yarn needs to be comfortable, pliable, and easily worked on knitting needles. It needs to be something we'd want to knit with *and* wear.

Cotton, for example, can make lovely socks if it's knit on machines at an extraordinarily fine gauge. Those machines

work their magic by modifying stitches to add bounce and elasticity where there is none in the fiber itself. But when you increase the yarn to a thickness more appropriate for handknitters, our ability to modify the stitches to create bounce and elasticity is diminished. And while you *can* knit socks out of any thickness of yarn, at a certain point each stitch becomes so pronounced that it may irritate the foot when stepped on—unless, perhaps, you're looking for this kind of self-massaging sock. For our purposes, a good sock yarn needs to be of a thickness and texture that we'd actually want to hold and work with, and yet it also needs to be something that will wear well. It needs to have sufficient bulk and loft to cushion our foot as we walk, and above all, it needs to be comfortable.

Let the Mystery Be

And, finally, the real kicker. No matter how much we try to study the science of fibers, yarns, and fabrics, a little bit of mystery remains for which there is no rational, scientific answer. Why can two skeins of the same yarn behave differently? We don't always know. We weren't at the farm when the thunder scared the sheep, causing them to develop a natural break in their fleece that ended up in a larger batch of fibers that were spun into yarn that, in your socks, wore out more quickly than it should have. Likewise, we weren't at the mill when the operator turned up the dial just a little so that he could leave in time for his daughter's birthday party. And we weren't at the Department of Public Works the day the operators changed their water treatment formula in such a way that the local hand-dyer's blue became faintly greener.

There are things we simply cannot know. While we can try to learn as much as possible to mitigate the risks—which is my goal with this book—there will always be a small magical component of knitting that must remain a mystery. The sooner we surrender to it, the more we can let go and enjoy the adventure.

Fiber Foundations

If yarn were a person, its skeletal system would be made entirely of fiber. This fine material gives strength, structure, and stability to all it touches, dictating how each skein, stitch, and sock will behave. Change the fibers in a yarn even slightly and you'll notice a difference on your foot.

Fibers play an important role in how a sock feels, fits, and lasts, which is why we'll look briefly at the most common fibers you're likely to find in a sock yarn. I want you to understand how each of these fibers meets (or doesn't meet) our need for elasticity, abrasion resistance, and moisture management.

Molecules Matter

The secret to fiber lies in the tiny threadlike molecules that lurk right beneath the surface. All fibers—whether from animals, plants, or synthetic materials—are made of these molecules. How the molecules are positioned and behave within the fiber dictates much of what we care about in a sock, from how it feels to how strong it is, from how it reacts to moisture to how much it can stretch before snapping.

Sometimes, as with wool, the molecules meander back and forth ever so slightly. Even when the wool fiber is pulled taut, its molecules still have room to stretch out further— which is what gives wool its exceptional elasticity. Such an arrangement tends to allow more moisture to penetrate and reside within the fiber without our feeling it. Other times, as with nylon, the molecules have already been so finely stretched that they are completely straight, extraordinarily strong, but arranged so densely that moisture barely has room to penetrate—so it stays on the fiber surface and we feel it a lot sooner. And then seed fibers, such as cotton, are strong and rigid even though their molecules are organized into spiral fibrils whose abundant open spaces invite moisture to take up residence. But the strength of seed fibers pales in comparison to that of bast fibers, such as linen, whose tightly aligned molecules can resist tremendous force before snapping—but whose inelasticity poses challenges in socks. As I said, molecules matter.

The Language of Sock Fibers

Many fiber qualities can impact a sock, but three stand out in particular: staple length, surface structure, and fineness. Each plays its part in constructing (or destroying) a perfectly good sock yarn.

STAPLE LENGTH

The average length of a fiber, when it's ready to be spun into yarn, is called *staple*. With a general understanding of staple lengths, you can look at a sock yarn and get a sense of whether or not it has sufficient twist to hold the fibers together under abrasion. Shorter fibers, such as Merino or cashmere, require more twist to hold together, but—at least in the animal world—these fibers tend to be among the softest and most desirable. To compensate for their fineness and short staple, such fibers are often blended with nylon for strength.

The longer the staple, the better it will resist abrasion for one simple reason: Longer fibers create fewer points of vulnerability along the length of your yarn. Their ends are few and deeply anchored. Shorter fibers begin and end more frequently, offering more ends that can come loose, get enmeshed with one another, and ultimately work their way out of the fabric in pills. Manufactured fibers, such as Tencel, nylon, and polyester, are born as infinite streams that are later solidified and chopped into artificial staple lengths to suit the needs of the yarn manufacturer—but they tend to be reasonably long.

SURFACE STRUCTURE

The world of yarn is a crowded one, with fibers jammed up against one another and constantly jostling for attention. How they interact with one another—and, ultimately, how they hold up on your foot—depends greatly on what their surface looks like. The smoother the fiber surface, the more easily the fibers will slide away from one another. The more textured the surface, the more entangled the fibers will become and the less likely they are to slip from one another's grasp. We like entanglement because it leads to a cohesive knitted fabric that will withstand lots of abrasion without failing.

Fiber gets its structure partly from its *crimp*, or its natural curl and wave pattern. Lots of crimp (called *high crimp*) is a desirable quality in fibers for sock yarn because it produces a bulky fabric with loft and padding. Picture a crowded elevator, with each fiber rubbing up against its neighbor. The finer and more numerous the crimps (as in Merino), the more the fibers resist one another and maintain their own distinct, springy identity—and the fewer fibers you'll need to fill the elevator. As an added bonus, when still air is

The length of a fiber dictates how much twist it needs to hold together in a yarn and, ultimately, in a sock.

The natural crimp pattern in fibers impacts how those fibers will sit together in yarn.

Finer fibers, such as this Mongolian cashmere, feel fabulous against our skin but are innately more fragile and susceptible to wear in socks.

trapped in yarn, it produces a warmer and more insulating fabric. But as the crimps get larger and more open, the fibers have fewer means with which to resist one another. They stand together more closely, allowing you to pack the elevator with many more fibers. In yarn terms, smoother fibers produce a dense and fluid yarn—the most typical example being a yarn made from 100 percent silk. Fluidity is fantastic in lace shawls, which exist to drape and adorn. But it's not such an ideal quality in socks, which need to hug and hold. Therefore, crimp is a good thing for sock yarns.

FINENESS

Our third essential fiber quality is fineness. In the animal-fiber world, fineness is dictated by the fiber diameter, which is measured in microns. The lower the number, the finer the fiber. One micron is one-millionth of a meter, or $3.93700787402 \times 10^{-5}$ inches, about the thickness of a very fine soap bubble. Cashmere, considered one of the finest protein fibers, averages 16 microns. A good Merino ranges from 17 to 22 microns, while the longer, stronger-wearing mediumwools will run anywhere from 24 to 31 microns. Manufactured fibers can be as fine as we want, since we control their diameter. The finest synthetic fibers measure 1 micron in diameter and are called *microfiber*.

Fineness tells us not only how soft and luscious our socks will feel against our skin but also warns us about potential weaknesses, especially in fibers that animals produce. Like china, the finer the fiber, the more fragile and susceptible it is to wear—and the more twist and strengthening stitches will be helpful to hold it together (all of which we'll talk about in coming chapters).

Now that we've added staple length, surface structure, and fineness to the mix, let's take a quick walk through some of the most common fibers you'll find in commercial sock yarns. I've grouped the sock-fiber world into four basic categories: fibers from animals (called *protein fibers*), fibers from plants (cotton being the most common), fibers that are manufactured from the regenerated cellulose in plants (bamboo and Tencel are two lustrous examples), and fibers that are manufactured entirely from synthetic materials (the most popular such fiber for socks being nylon).

Protein Fibers

THE SECRETS OF SCALES

In protein fibers, another quality adds structure to yarn: the microscopic overlapping scales that cover the surface of each fiber. Scales protect the inner fiber and monitor what goes in and comes out—letting moisture come and go when the climate dictates. The larger the scales, the smoother the fiber surface and the shinier it may appear to the eye. The smaller the scales, the more interruptions along the fiber surface and the more matte it may appear. It's akin to the way the surface of a pond may look smooth on still days and matte on windy ones. Scales also provide essential friction among fibers to help them stay in place when under abrasion.

Just as bamboo needles are less slippery than nickel-plated steel ones, a fiber surface that's covered with tiny scales (such as Merino) is less slippery than a completely smooth surface (such as silk). Since socks are subject to an extreme amount of back-and-forth abrasion, we want fibers that won't slip away from one another when rubbed. Which is why scales are a sock-knitter's friend.

Protein fibers are grown by animals, and the mother of all protein fibers is wool. This category also includes everything from alpacas and llamas to angora goats, cashmere goats, angora rabbits, and even the noble Arctic musk ox. If an animal grew it and you want to knit with it, chances are it's a protein fiber.

As diverse as these animals are, their fibers are even more so. Some are short, others long; some have robust curls, others have tiny accordion folds; some look matte in the light, others shine like glass. Even the word *wool* is just the beginning of a vast and intriguing journey. Like restaurants in San Francisco, you could knit with a different protein fiber every day and never grow bored.

But despite their diversity, protein fibers do share some common, underlying characteristics that are particularly welcome in socks. They are extremely warm and absorbent, offering the very moisture-management properties we need most by our feet. They tend to be resilient and highly elastic (some more than others), allowing the sock to stretch and easily return to its original shape. And, when spun with sufficient twist, they can offer sufficient abrasion resistance for most of our sock needs.

SHEEP

All protein fibers have a crimp pattern that varies from animal to animal. Wool fibers run the gamut from short (2 inches [5cm]) to extremely long (12 inches

[30.5cm] or more), with crimp ranging from fine to large ringlets and even wild corkscrew spirals, all depending on which breed of sheep grew the wool. Delicate finewools, such as Merino, have the tiniest, most regular crimps that zigzag evenly along the fiber, like the folds of an accordion. They can have anywhere from 14 to 30 crimps per inch

SOCKS AND MACHINE-WASHABLE WOOLS

As helpful as scales are in keeping our socks intact, they do have a dark side—one that's usually only discovered after you toss your beloved wool sock in a washing machine full of hot, soapy water. As they absorb water, which they love to do, protein fibers swell and the ends of those tiny scales begin to pop out from the fiber surface. Once the washing machine begins to agitate, the scales touch one another and become irretrievably enmeshed. By the end of the rinse cycle, your beloved sock will only fit a squirrel. When done intentionally, the process is called felting or fulling. When done unintentionally, it's usually called a disaster.

This is why yarn companies offer machine-washable wool yarns. Specific fiber treatments vary, but the most common technique for making machine-washable wool is to expose the wool fibers to an enzyme that eats the tiny outer edges off the scales. With nothing to pop out and enmesh during washing, the wool can withstand routine dunks in a washing machine without ill effect. But some machine-washable wool fibers have been rendered so smooth that they lack sufficient surface friction to hold together in the wash. The fibers slide easily from one another's grasp and make the fabric stretch. The only way to find out if your sock will stretch twice its length in the wash is to knit a swatch, wash it, and then hang it to dry under a small amount of tension. If it doesn't stretch, you're in good shape. Wool is currently the only protein fiber that is commercially treated for machine-washability in yarn, and nearly all machine-washable fiber processing takes place in China.

(2.5cm). The vast majority of sock yarns on the market are made from Merino. All's the pity, because many other sheep breeds—such as Columbia, Corriedale, Finnish Landrace, and Tunis—have a lovely feel, good staple length, and great strength that make them far better for socks. But those breeds lack the soft succulence we've come to expect in yarn, and they tend to be harder to source in large quantities. If you find these yarns at fiber festivals or from small farm vendors, do give them a try.

ALPACA

Another popular protein fiber is alpaca, whose natural crimp pattern can range from reasonably fine to open and large, depending on the age and type of animal. Alpaca tends to be smooth, dense, warm, and—some will argue—overpowering for socks when used at 100 percent. Alpaca benefits from a healthy percentage of wool to open up the mix and give the sock yarn some welcome elasticity.

MOHAIR

The same is true for mohair, which grows in long, glorious ringlets from the angora goat. On its own, mohair can be too dense and slippery for socks. But at 10–20 percent, it's an excellent natural strengthening alternative to nylon, and it adds a stunning silklike shine.

Also remember that the younger the animal, the finer its fibers will be. If you've been sensitive to some mohair yarns in the past, for example, look for the words *kid* or *baby kid* on the label. (Likewise, with alpaca look for the word *baby*.) The flip side of choosing finer fibers is that they'll be weaker and more vulnerable to abrasion. It's all about trade-offs and choosing what's important to you personally.

LUXURY FIBERS: CASHMERE, BISON, YAK, AND QIVIUT

Where do the true luxury fibers—such as cashmere, bison, yak, and qiviut—fall in the sock mix? These delicate down undercoat fibers tend to be extremely short with a fine and somewhat chaotic crimp. Rarely, if ever, will you find these fibers used at 100 percent in sock yarns—they simply lack sufficient strength and elasticity to do the job well. (Here I'm referring to commercially available yarns. Handspinners have an advantage because they can spin the fibers properly for optimal sock performance.) But in wool blends or when sufficiently reinforced with nylon (as you can see in Marlaina Bird's Buddleia on page 95), down fibers can lend a glorious halo, softness, and extraordinary insulating

BLENDS AND THE 5 PERCENT RULE

Yarn companies blend fibers by weight, not volume. By their very nature, finer fibers weigh less—meaning that a 10 percent addition of cashmere gives you far more fiber than would 10 percent of a denser fiber, such as mohair.

Still, some argue that when the fiber content gets down to 5 percent or less, one fiber is indistinguishable from the next, so it shouldn't even get credit on the label. To this end, under the Textile and Wool Acts, the Federal Trade Commission requires that any blend containing less than 5 percent of a fiber other than wool should list that fiber simply as "other fiber" or "other fibers." (Interestingly enough, other protein fibers, such as cashmere, are also housed under the "wool" label.) The only exceptions are those fibers that have a definite functional significance, such as spandex for elasticity, nylon for strength, or sterling silver for sparkle (which you can see in Melissa Morgan-Oakes's Tutu on page 114). I know of only one commercial yarn company that adheres to this rule, but it's a good rule to understand nonetheless. When you see *other* on the label, you don't necessarily need to worry that the yarn company has put shredded cardboard or used milk cartons in the yarn—it's simply following FTC guidelines.

power. Several popular sock yarns contain 10–20 percent cashmere for precisely these reasons.

ANGORA

Another excellent blend candidate is angora, which comes to us from the angora rabbit. On their own, the short, slippery fibers need far more twist for socks than most millspun angora yarns

provide. But in wool blends, a dusting of 10 percent angora will do the trick perfectly.

Silk

A hybrid fiber that could be considered both plant and animal, silk is made from the digested cellulose of mulberry leaves that the humble silkworm extrudes when forming its cocoon. Unlike its four-legged-grown counterparts, silk is an extraordinarily smooth, glassy material with no surface scales or crimp whatsoever. Right out of the gate, its molecules are tightly packed and aligned in the overall direction of the fiber, with no meandering back and forth to give added elasticity. Reeled straight from the cocoon, each silk fiber can be as long as 800 yards (731.5m), but those longer fibers tend to be reserved for the high-fashion textiles market. Most silk in handknitting yarns has been cut into shorter lengths for spinning.

Silk is warm and absorbent, with much greater strength than wool or cotton. But it loses several points on the sock scale because of its relative inelasticity—far less than wool, but more than cotton. The lack of crimp creates a very dense, fluid yarn with spectacular drape but no bounce. Silk makes a great addition to wool sock yarns at 10–20 percent, giving strength, warmth, and luster without overpowering wool's loft and elasticity. Just be aware that the more silk you add, the denser and less elastic the yarn will become.

Plant Fibers

Plant fibers come to us from two sources: seeds (such as cotton) and stalks (such as linen and hemp). In both cases, these fibers are composed almost entirely of cellulose and are extremely strong, rigid, and absorbent.

SEED FIBERS

The typical plant fiber used in sock yarns is cotton, though it's rarely used at 100 percent. Cotton has no scales along the fiber surface, but it does twist in microscopic contortions similar to those of a dried vanilla bean. These contortions create a surface structure that helps hold the fibers together reasonably well, though not with quite as much cohesion as wool. Cotton also has fantastic moisture-management properties, wicking moisture away from the skin so that it can evaporate and keep the wearer cool. And, unlike protein fibers, which weaken when wet, cotton actually becomes stronger when exposed to moisture.

Despite all these positive qualities, cotton is rarely used on its own in sock yarns. Cotton lacks the fundamental elasticity that we require for a well-wearing pair of handknitted socks. The hosiery industry can work magic with its tighter-spun finer-gauge yarns and plush, machine-manipulated fabrics, but when the cotton yarn reaches a thickness that's comfortable for handknitting, it often becomes too dense and unyielding to produce a springy fabric. Socks knit out of 100 percent cotton will need to be reblocked after each wear, and they will gradually lose their ability to return to their original shape after blocking.

If you love the feel of cotton, consider a yarn that blends up to 50 percent cotton with wool. This is one of the most felicitous fiber blends possible, whether for socks or other garments, because each fiber perfectly complements the other, helping it overcome its weaknesses without overpowering the blend. Among the many types of cotton that grow around the world, Sea Island and Egyptian cottons are the strongest. Also, mercerized cotton is stronger and much more lustrous than standard cotton, but it will be smoother and thus, from a sock-yarn perspective, much more dense and inelastic. If wool is completely out of the question, seek a mix that contains up to 5 percent spandex or another form of elastic. Also remember that cotton fibers tend to be extremely short, so choose a yarn with sufficient twist to hold these short fibers together under abrasion.

BAST FIBERS

 Fibers can also be derived from the stalks of plants, the best known of which are linen (which comes from the flax plant) and hemp. Called *bast fibers*, these are among the oldest recorded fibers used by

Silk, while too inelastic on its own for socks, adds welcome luster and strength to wool blends, such as the one used in version B of Melissa Morgan-Oakes's Tutu (shown here and on page 114).

Bast fibers, such as linen or mechanically processed bamboo (shown here in Stephen Houghton's Salted Caramels, and on page 77), add a natural strengthening alternative to nylon while also giving a touch of luster.

humans, and for good reason: They're extremely strong and absorbent, and they become even more beautiful and lustrous with wear. Their only shortcoming is that they have no elasticity whatsoever. For this reason, they're best used sparingly—at 10–25 percent—to add natural strength to wool blends. More than 25 percent and the fibers will start to overpower the fabric and lower its elasticity.

Among the lesser-known bast fibers is bamboo—not the soft, shiny stuff we see everywhere, but the stronger, sturdier fiber that is actually made from the stalk of the bamboo plant in much the same way that we obtain linen and hemp. Look for the words *mechanically processed* bamboo on the yarn label, but be prepared to hunt. This form of bamboo remains relatively rare in the yarn world. Zitron Trekking Pro Natura is the best-known example to date, and you can see this 75 percent wool, 25 percent bamboo blend in Stephen Houghton's Salted Caramels on page 77. Note that the Trekking Pro Natura label describes its bamboo as *unprocessed*, but technically the fiber *did* get processed into yarn—just mechanically, not chemically.

Regenerated Cellulose

Marvels of modern technology and chemical engineering, regenerated cellulose fibers are made from the naturally occurring cellulose in plants. Through a lengthy chemical process, this cellulose is chopped up and dissolved into a liquid that is processed and eventually extruded into a bath of acid that turns the goo back into solid form—only this time, instead of a branch or a stalk, it's a slender strand of fiber.

Whether from bamboo or birch trees or any cellulose-producing plant in between, all regenerated cellulose fibers share the same fundamental traits. They are smooth and lustrous, absorbent and warm, stronger than wool but weaker than silk, with even less elasticity than cotton. For our sock purposes, regenerated cellulose fibers should be used sparingly and only in blends to provide luster and warmth, if needed. These fibers lack sufficient crimp or surface texture—*any*, as a matter of fact—to adhere to one another in yarn. Twist can only do so much. With sufficient wear, the fibers in a 100 percent–regenerated cellulose garment will slip from one another and cause the fabric to stretch significantly (usually in whatever direction gravity happens to be pulling). This is true even with yarns knit at a tighter sock gauge.

Of all the regenerated cellulose fibers on the market, Tencel (the U.S. name for lyocell) is the strongest. It's also the cleanest, with a solvent spinning process that recovers and recycles some 99 percent of the amine oxide solvents that are used during manufacturing.

If you've fallen passionately in love with a 100 percent–regenerated cellulose yarn, don't despair—simply consider it for a shawl or scarf that can drape and stretch to its heart's content. If you want regenerated cellulose in your socks, seek a blend in the 10–20 percent range, making sure that the remaining fibers have plenty of elasticity in them. If the percentage of regenerated cellulose fiber is higher, consider a sock pattern whose stitches will also add elasticity to the mix.

Synthetic Fibers

All the fibers in this category are man-made using synthetic resins that were ultimately derived from coal. They are the strongest of all the fibers discussed thus far and just as durable. They're also warm and well-wearing.

Why don't we knit all our socks out of synthetic fibers, then? Besides the fact that synthetic fibers are not biodegradable, they also have the lowest moisture regain of any fiber we've talked about thus far. These fibers are essentially solid tubes of material—no scales, no nothing. During manufacturing, we can stretch these fibers so that their inner molecules are ramrod straight and completely aligned for strength, and we can steam-set them with various crimp patterns, but we can't do anything about the fact that, ultimately, these fibers want nothing to do with moisture. This is why static cling became such an issue in the 1950s and 1960s—for the first time in history, we were dressing ourselves in fabrics that did not breathe. And socks need to breathe.

Still, synthetic fibers have their moments. They tend to be the most affordable yarn option, though not always. And they have the easiest care requirements (just pop them in the washing machine and walk away). They're useful as well-wearing gifts for the handwash-weary and, likewise, can be suitable choices when knitting for charities that ask you to use easy-care materials.

ELASTIC YARN, TENSION, AND GAUGE

The more elastic a yarn contains, the trickier gauge and tension may be. We've been trained to hold our yarn under tension as we knit—and tension is the enemy of elastic. It'll do everything within its power to absorb that energy so that we don't feel it. You'll need to swatch and determine where you want the fabric to be in terms of gauge, and then play with needle size and tension techniques until you find a comfortable approach you can maintain for an entire project.

NYLON

Among all the synthetic fibers you're likely to find in sock yarn, nylon (also called Polyamid) has the greatest strength and abrasion resistance. It's often added to wool for reinforcement, especially in sock yarns. The two fibers share similar chemical structures, both being essentially long polypeptide chains that offer similar elasticity and extensibility. Mills also love blending nylon with wool because it improves the spinning efficiency of wool, allowing them to spin it finer without breaking. Because nylon shares the extremely low (and/or nonexistent) regain of other synthetic fibers, it's best kept at 10–20 percent in socks. Any more than this and you'll begin to feel a sticky quality in the yarn.

POLYESTER AND ACRYLIC

Polyester also fares well in terms of abrasion resistance and strength, but it has only adequate pilling resistance. Acrylic isn't quite as strong as polyester, and its resistance to abrasion is slightly lower, but it makes up for these shortcomings with a more natural, "wooly" hand that more closely mimics the bulk and loft of wool. Lacking scales along their fiber surface, however, all three synthetic fibers are prone to pilling.

LYCRA

A final synthetic fiber that's particularly friendly for socks is elastic, frequently called spandex or referred to by the Invista-trademarked name, Lycra. A mere 1–5 percent is all you need to add sufficient elasticity to most inelastic fibers, including cotton and bamboo. Above 10 percent, your socks will start to feel like support stockings—which may or may not be what you want.

With this map of the fiber world in hand, I hope you have a better understanding of why and how fiber can, indeed, make a difference in the finished sock. But the adventure doesn't stop here. Let's see what happens when we choose our fibers and head off to the mill.

3

The Yarns

Twist is energy. It's the vital life force, the connective tissue that holds our yarn skeleton together. The more twist in a yarn, the more energy is holding fibers together. The less twist, the less energy. If you push twist too far, it will eventually weaken the fiber and cause the yarn to snap. But up to that very moment, twist is it. And out of all the garments that need this kind of energy to hold together, socks rank first.

Getting Twist Right

Why don't yarn manufacturers simply twist the heck out of all their yarns and call it a day? Twist isn't quite that easy. The tighter it is, the firmer the yarn becomes; and the firmer the yarn, the less pliable and pleasant it is to work with and wear. Conversely, the looser the twist, the softer and more comfortable the yarn—but with less energy holding it together, the sooner the yarn will start to wear. Yarn companies constantly strive to hit that sweet spot between too tight and too loose because nobody wants to wear a pair of socks knit out of piano wire, no matter how strong it might be.

WHY WORSTED SPINNING WORKS FOR SOCKS

Nearly all the socks in this book were knit using yarns that were spun in either the worsted or semiworsted spinning method. (*Worsted* can also refer to a particular thickness of yarn, but that's not what I'm talking about here.) The reason nearly all sock yarns are spun worsted is simple: The worsted spinning method creates the strongest, most durable yarn—and for everyday socks, we need strength and durability.

Worsted spinning involves combing all the fibers into perfect alignment, with any short or irregular fibers being removed in the process. The more completely the fibers overlap and the more tightly the ends are tucked in, the better the resulting yarn will resist abrasion. Hence, worsted spinning works well for socks.

How do yarn manufacturers know how much twist a yarn needs? They start, or I wish they would, with staple length. As we discussed in the last chapter, the longer the fiber, the fewer twists required to hold each inch of fibers in place (or each centimeter, for our metric friends). The shorter the fiber, the more twists per inch. It's an embarrassingly simple baseline, but it's a helpful start for socks. Fiber blends are often conceived to allow shorter fibers to be spun more loosely, the assumption being that the longer fibers will hold everything in check. Sometimes they do hold everything together, especially with intimate blends in which the fibers are nearly indistinguishable from one another. But sometimes they don't.

I'm a firm believer in finding creative solutions that let us heed the call of a beautiful yarn, regardless of how it was spun. Take Jared Flood's Strago (page 150) as an example. The socks are made from a lofty and jumbled woolen-spun wool that might not hold up very well if you jammed it in a shoe and wore it to work every day. But knit at a double thickness (for colorwork) and designed for padding around home on a wintry night, it's warm, wooly, and perfectly appropriate.

The act of plying gives mills even more leeway in terms of providing sufficient twist to fibers while producing a supple, willing yarn. Here's how it works.

Singles

The basic building block for all yarn is the single continuous  strand of twisted fibers—so unintended for solo use that it's referred to in the plural as *singles*. If twist is energy, then singles are the most illogical solution for handknitted socks because the fibers have the least amount of energy holding them together.

Still, a few daring yarn companies have tried to offer singles sock yarns. Most of them, such as those from Noro, feature stunning color variegation. The biggest problem to date with singles sock yarns has been wearability—even though these so-called singles are actually composed of at least two finer strands that have been given a hint of twist before being spun together into what looks like a singles. Mills have further compensated for the innate weakness of singles by giving the yarns an unusually high nylon content, which has increased their wearability somewhat but, in the process, has reduced the yarn's ability to breathe.

Compounding the wearability problem is the fact that singles can only be spun so tight before all that extra twist causes the fabric to bias. In socks, which are knit in the round, the fabric will slant in a corkscrewlike fashion.

Sometimes this effect can be pretty, but it does pose problems for any stitch patterns that rely on your stitches lining up vertically.

What to do with all those pretty singles sock yarns, then? I vote that you bypass the wearability issue altogether by

Singles offer the least strength of any sock yarn. To compensate, many yarn manufacturers add higher quantities of nylon (such as the 30% nylon used in Noro Kureyon Sock, shown here).

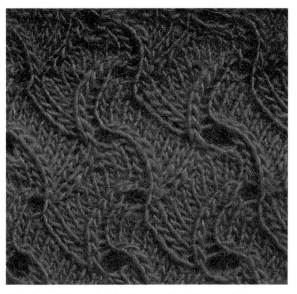

Singles with gradual color variegation, such as Schoppel Wolle Zauberball used in version B of Cirilia Rose's Prana (page 144), are ideal for large areas of low-abrasion fabric such as legs and cuffs.

using them for lower-abrasion gear like leg warmers and Cirilia Rose's Prana (page 144), which have no heel or toe at all. As an added bonus, both types of projects also offer larger fabric real estate that's ideal for showing off any color variegation in the yarn.

Two Plies

Once we twist strands of spun fiber together into yarn, a whole world of possibility opens up. (Note that when I say *ply*, I'm referring to the number of physical strands that are twisted together into yarn, not the system of yarn weight that is still used in some parts of the world.)

When strands of spun fiber are twisted together into yarn, they create a ply structure that can show up as tiny shadows in our knitting. The more strands plied together, the finer the shadows; the fewer the plies, the more pronounced the shadows become. This is especially true in two-ply yarns, whose dueling strands operate rather like airplane propellers, constantly rotating and holding open far more space at any given time than their fibers actually

occupy. With the two plies constantly pushing away from each other, two-ply yarns engage in a dance of yarn and air, occupied and unoccupied space. These are the flat-tipped calligraphy pens of the yarn world.

Buddleia (left, and on page 95) and version B of Veil of Rosebuds (right, and on page 102) show how a two-ply yarn can go from fuzzy to distinct depending on the fibers and ply angle.

Classic Elite Alpaca Sox and its relaxed two plies.

RELAXED TWO-PLY YARN

When two strands are twisted together gently in a relaxed, languid fashion, the resulting yarn, stitches, and sock will all be reasonably fluid. The ply shadows will still be visible though somewhat minimized, flickering quietly in the background. Such a yarn is a better choice for sock patterns in which you want some stitch clarity without too much shadow interruption. But just remember that the lower the twist, the less energy is holding the fibers together. If you tend to be tough on socks, be wary of using such a yarn for patterns that have minimal heel structure—or consider swapping any vulnerable stockinette heel for a thicker slipped-stitch heel instead.

TIGHTLY TWISTED TWO-PLY YARN

On the other hand, if the component strands are twisted together at such a tight angle that they almost appear perpendicular to the overall direction of the yarn, the resulting yarn will be much stronger and springier. It will also display more spunk and personality on the needles, producing far deeper ply shadows that give knitted fabric a cobblestoned effect. This trait is particularly intriguing in smaller stitch motifs and innately bumpy designs that incorporate knit and purl stitches.

Yak fibers in Marlaina Bird's Buddleia (page 95) create a halo that conceals some of the ply shadows normally visible in a two-ply yarn.

Madelinetosh Tosh Sock and its springy, almost perpendicular two plies.

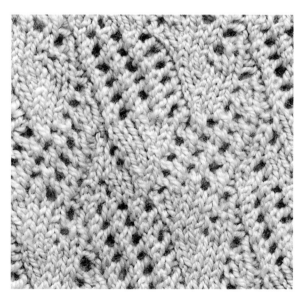

Smooth and springy two-ply yarns give shadow and nuance to stitch patterns, such as the Veil of Rosebuds (page 100) shown here in Madelinetosh Tosh Sock.

Certain types of fibers will behave differently in two-ply yarns. For example, those fibers with a tendency to create a halo, such as the yak in Marlaina Bird's Buddleia (page 95), will conceal most of the ply shadows of a two-ply yarn, no matter how tight the twist or how high the ply angle. Smoother and shinier fibers will give any shadows far greater clarity, as you can see in both versions of Anne Hanson's Veil of Rosebuds (page 100).

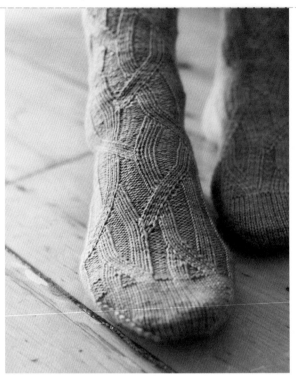

Three-ply yarns can render broad brushstrokes of stockinette motifs (such as those in Cookie A's Elm on page 72, knit in String Theory Caper Sock) with smooth, calligraphic detail.

Three plies in Swans Island Organic Merino have been twisted together at a medium angle, giving softness, fluidity, and cohesive stitch definition.

Three plies in Quince & Co. Tern have been twisted together at a perpendicular angle for greater bounce and strength.

Three Plies

Now it's getting fun. While the strands in our two-ply yarn were in a pitched battle for independence, the strands in a three-ply yarn nest together in a perfectly contented state. Three-ply yarns are, like the three-legged stool that doesn't wobble, incredibly stable materials. For well-wearing socks, who could want more?

Three-ply yarns render a smooth stockinette with good stitch definition and fine ply shadows—the yarn equivalent of writing with a nice felt-tip pen. Their relative roundedness makes them especially well-suited for high-relief ribbing, cables, and cohesive colorwork. While lace tends to look prettiest in two-ply yarns, smaller and simpler lace motifs, such as those in Jayme Stahl's Isabella d'Este (page 107) can still be lovely in a three-ply yarn. The added energy of that third ply tends to make these yarns much stronger than their singles and two-ply counterparts, although the tightness of twist, fiber length, and angle of ply will still impact the yarn's overall strength and durability. The rounder structure of three- and more-ply yarns will also give greater cohesion and strength to your socks. They're also a great option when you want to create large, smooth stockinette motifs with minimal ply or shadow interruption, such as Cookie A's Elm (page 72), knit from a three-ply blend of Merino, cashmere, and nylon. Some sock knitters still prefer the added nuance of the pebbly two-ply fabric, but three-ply sock yarns are an excellent choice when you want a smooth, basic, well-defined and well-wearing fabric.

Four and More Plies

As we add even more plies to our yarn, we increase its ability to withstand wear and tear exponentially—  although, again, the fiber, tightness of twist, and even the fit of your shoe can still impact the finished product. With three or more plies, those plies will always want to nest. In four-ply yarns, this nesting instinct can inadvertently push out the fourth ply, forcing it to wander, lonely, around the outside of each stitch. (You'll only see this if you look really closely, but still . . . it's there.)

Each additional ply also gives yarn greater structure and resistance to compression—something that's helpful for socks that get trampled on all day long. Multiple-ply yarns produce a very clean, smooth stockinette with rounded stitches and extremely clear stitch definition. They render steady ribbing and lovely cables.

Smaller, simpler lace motifs can look cozy and cohesive in a three-ply yarn, such as the Spirit Trail Sunna used in Isabelle D'Este (page 107).

The four plies in Lang Jawoll Silk present a smooth, well-balanced yarn with durability, cohesion, and stitch clarity.

S-on-S Cables

Most of the large commercial mills spin fibers primarily for the textiles market, with our knitting market serving only as a convenient add-on. The textiles market relies on yarns of a far finer gauge than you or I would ever have the patience to knit on our needles. But when we take those fine strands and ply them together, and then ply those plied strands together, we begin to achieve a yarn thickness that is comfortable and useful for our own purposes.

S-on-S cabled yarn is made this way. It is composed of fine strands of yarn that are plied together in a counterclockwise direction, and then each of those two-ply strands is further plied together in the same counterclockwise direction.

If twist is energy, these yarns have the maximum amount. Made from elastic fibers, such as wool, S-on-S cabled yarns will be extremely springy and energetic, with the clearest and brightest possible stitch definition. They're often called "crepe" yarns because the ply shadows line up in a rippled, crepelike fashion in the knitted fabric.

Their roundedness helps S-on-S cabled yarns render cables in high, sculptural relief and even do beautiful things with knit and purl stitches—as you can see in Cat Bordhi's Darjeeling (page 61). This same roundedness makes S-on-S cabled yarns less suited to colorwork, because they lack the necessary surface halo to fill gaps between stitches and blend the colors for a cohesive picture. It's the difference between drawing a landscape with a felt-tipped pen or a smooth rollerball. But for all other purposes, S-on-S cabled yarns create perfectly strong and durable socks.

There is one thing you should know about these yarns, if you don't already. By virtue of all the twist running in the

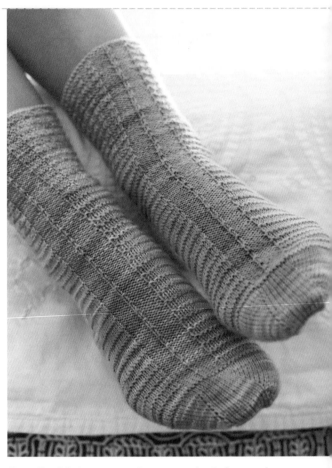

S-on-S cabled yarns render textured stitches, such as the purl motifs in Cat Bordhi's Darjeeling (page 61), with high relief and crisp definition.

counterclockwise direction, these yarns cause the left leg of your knit stitch to stand upright at attention (instead of relaxed in the normal V stance). It's not your fault, and there's not much you can do about it but pretend it was intentional.

True Cables

When we take those same fine component plies and ply them together in the opposite direction of their original ply, we end up with a true cabled yarn. The simple act of reversing that twist during the final plying stage locks the plies together, creating a strong, smooth, well-balanced yarn with a ton of structure and stability. It renders a perfectly even stockinette without that pesky upright left leg, and its shadows show up only as tiny speckles, rather like a piece of coral.

While cable-spun yarns can create beautiful stockinette, they excel in textured stitchwork, especially cables. The true cable-spun yarn that Norah Gaughan used for Rocaille (page 89) renders the cables with the fullness and clarity that you'd expect to see in the freshly piped frosting on a birthday cake.

The only drawback in terms of using these yarns for socks is elasticity. When spun from high-elasticity fibers, such as wool or polyester, they'll do fine. But when spun from low-elasticity fibers, such as cotton, cable-spun yarns can be too ropelike and unyielding for socks. If you've fallen for such a yarn and still want to use it, be sure to find a sock pattern whose cuff has plenty of elastic stitches in it, such as ribbing, or opt for a sock pattern with an intentionally slouchy cuff.

Core-Spun

As the name suggests, core-spun yarns are made from plied strands of fiber  that are literally wrapped around a core fiber. This technique is ideal for concealing a structural fiber, such as elastic. Because the surrounding fibers are wrapped at a near-perpendicular angle, they can stretch much more than if they were twisted in a standard three- or four-ply fashion. This allows them to move freely with the elastic that's inside. Rounded and strong, core-spun yarns can be a clever solution for knitters who want to work with cooler, low-elasticity fibers, like cotton, but still want spring in their socks.

Fiber, twist, and ply create the very foundation of what we care about in our socks. But with clever use of our needles, we can still make small adjustments to enhance or overcome any issues with the fibers and twist in our yarn, helping even the unlikely skein become a pair of lovely and useful socks for our feet. The secret lies in our stitches, and that's where we head next.

True cable-spun yarns render cables with sculptural fullness and clarity.

The plied strands of fiber in OnLine Supersocke Summer Cotton Stretch conceal a structural strand of elastic that runs down the yarn's center.

Stitch Tricks

Have you fallen in love with a yarn, only now to discover that it may not be the best choice for socks? Or maybe you've already used the right yarns but your soles *still* keep wearing thin. With a little work up front, we still may be able to make your sock dreams come true.

We can't always work total magic with our needles, but we can make subtle adjustments that will accommodate any known shortcomings of a yarn and add even more strength and elasticity to those yarns we already know are good. I've sorted these tips and variables into broad categories, keeping in mind that some can be used for multiple purposes. Don't be afraid to experiment and see what works best for you. The more familiar you are with your options, the more readily you'll be able to pull them out of your bag of tricks and put them to good use.

Tricks for Elasticity

Knitted fabric is, by its very nature, an elastic material. It is formed from rows upon rows of interlocking loops, each of which allows for stretch and movement. Still, some stitches and stitch combinations will provide for more elasticity than others.

RIBBING

The simplest and fastest way to add elasticity to any yarn or sock is to introduce ribbing. When knits and purls are stacked on top of one another, they form elastic columns of fabric that willingly stretch to accommodate many kinds of legs.

If we stagger those knits and purls so that the columns never get formed, we end up with a looser fabric that stretches nicely but doesn't have quite the same degree of

> *The simplest and fastest way to add elasticity to any yarn or sock is to introduce ribbing.*

elastic return as standard ribbing. Such a fabric is ideal for slouchy socks. Designers will sometimes compromise by placing a length of regular ribbing along the top of the cuff before switching to a looser stitch for the leg.

If you're knitting for a friend and aren't sure of his or her calf circumference, steer clear of any highly tailored, low-elasticity kneesocks. Instead, look for patterns that combine columns of knit and purl stitches along the cuff and leg. The more frequent the columns are, the more elastic the fabric will be. Some maintain that k1/p1 produces the most elastic fabric, then k2/p2, and onward, with each additional stitch reducing the elasticity by a certain degree. But Elizabeth Zimmermann insists that k2/p2 ribbing is the most elastic of all, and who would argue with Elizabeth?

The cuff in Anne Hanson's Veil of Rosebuds (left, and on page 100) gets welcome elasticity from yarn-over increases, while Jane Cochran's Hickory (right, and on page 66) relies on columns of knits and purls for its stretchiness.

STRETCHY INCREASES

How we work increases also impacts the elasticity of our fabric. Increasing by knitting through the front and back of each stitch creates a firm, relatively inconspicuous increase that jams two stitches into a space where only one existed before. Fabric with these kinds of increases, especially when they are stacked directly on top of one another, can be rather dense and inelastic, especially since the increases will need to be paired with innately inelastic decreases. A slightly more elastic increase can be formed by picking up and knitting into the strand that runs between the stitch you've just worked and the next one on your needle—although this increase will also be more visible.

The most elastic increase comes from working a yarn-over, or essentially wrapping the yarn around the needle to create a new stitch. Yarn-overs produce a nice, stretchy, open hole in our fabric. Anne Hanson uses this technique to create the mesh openwork in her Veil of Rosebuds (page 100). Obviously, we'll want to think twice about swapping one increase for another in any pattern, since each is used for a very specific design effect, but we can study the stitches in potential sock patterns to get a decent sense of how elastic the fabric is going to be. If you know the pattern won't have much elasticity, double-check to make sure that your yarn will have sufficient springiness to compensate—or choose another yarn that's better suited to the task.

THE CABLE CONUNDRUM

Most traditional cable patterns are set against a backdrop of purl stitches. The presence of orderly knit and purl stitches might lead one to conclude that all cable patterns are equally elastic, but they are not. The smaller the cables,

In Firefly (page 84), Jennifer Hagan staggered small cable motifs among larger runs of knits and purls to keep the cuff elastic and comfortable.

the more elasticity they tend to allow in the fabric. The larger the cables, the less yielding the fabric may be.

Cables require more yarn than most other stitch patterns, creating a dense fabric that isn't always happy to be squished between foot and shoe. Also, the act of turning a cable causes the entire fabric to pull inwards in a way that does not want to stretch—or, rather, it *will* stretch while

Cookie A's Elm (page 72) uses clever increases and decreases to create the illusion of cables.

also stressing those vulnerable crossed stitches in the row where you turned the cable. You'll find several gorgeous cabled sock patterns in this book, so I'm obviously not against cables altogether. But I do want you to go into a cabled sock project with both eyes open. Cables are best worked in lighter-weight sock yarns whose fibers and/or twist will give the fabric lots of stretch.

FAUX CABLES

You can also use clever increases and decreases to create the *illusion* of cables while avoiding the potential density and inelasticity of true overlapping stitches. Cookie A uses this technique with particular skill in Elm (page 72). Not only does the stitch pattern produce an intriguing cablelike motif, but it does so while combining knits and purls for greater elasticity.

You can also use the faux-cable technique to transform standard vertical ribbing into a more gently undulating rib pattern that still has an excellent degree of elasticity. Jane Cochran uses this effect in Hickory (page 66), as does Stephen Houghton in his Salted Caramels (page 77).

Tricks for Strength

Woven fabric benefits from two strands of tightly interlacing yarn to give strength and durability, but knitted fabric is a purely monofilament creation. One strand of yarn is responsible for the fabric's entire strength and structure. Fortunately, just as we can adjust our stitches for greater elasticity, we can also make minor modifications in our stitches that will enhance the fabric's strength and its ability to withstand abrasion.

TWISTED STITCHES

Knitting through the back of a stitch instead of the front produces a twisted stitch that looks rather like a V with its legs crossed. The act of twisting a stitch pulls in the fabric ever so slightly, making this a helpful technique any time you need to make your fabric a little more snug. Just be aware that it changes the look of the stitch.

Twisted stitches are often used to "draw" fine pictures against a background of purls, as you see in Sivia Harding's Lady Tryamour (page 122). The presence of knits and purls gives the fabric reasonable elasticity, although the twisting of the knit stitches does make the socks more snug.

The concept of twisted stitches can go even further, as Nancy Bush demonstrates in Kensington (page 131). Instead of twisting individual stitches, she reversed the order in which pairs of stitches were knit to create twisting or crossed pairs of stitches—technically called "faux" cables. In this way, she drew an elaborate zigzagging latticework picture of traveling stitches. Regardless of whether you twist individual stitches or stitch pairs, you'll want to stick with yarns that have a high percentage of elastic fiber, such as wool, for maximum comfort and wearability.

Not all sock designers agree on the efficacy of twisted stitches, however. Charline Schurch maintains that the crisscrossing nature of twisted stitches will cause the fibers in each strand of yarn to saw into one another when under compression and abrasion, ultimately accelerating the failure of your sock.

SWAPPING SIZES AND TRIGGER-LOADING

Gauge matters in socks. It dictates durability. Unfortunately, we can't always count on a yarn label to indicate the ideal sock gauge for a yarn, because socks always want to be knit tighter than most other things you'd knit with that same yarn. Or, as Lucy Neatby puts it, "Socks should be worked on abnormally small needles for the size of the yarn." Because many yarn companies have the odd misconception that big numbers scare us, they tend to choose the smallest number when it comes to gauge (and larger numbers when it comes to needle size). While I

Crossing pairs of stitches in Kensington (left, and on page 131) and individual twisted stitches in Lady Tryamour (right, and on page 122) are useful techniques for keeping fabric snug.

Twisted stitches are also ideal for drawing fine "pictures," as Sivia Harding does in Lady Tryamour (page 122).

Fabric's gauge and density are impacted both by needle circumference and by the distance between the stitch just worked and the stitch about to be worked.

won't say that yarn labels lie, they can—like rose colored glasses or that cleverly doctored bathroom scale—present an inaccurate view of reality.

To produce a well-wearing sock, let these numbers be your guide. In fingering-weight yarn, your gauge should be between 8 and 10 stitches per inch (2.5cm); in a sport- or DK-weight yarn, keep your gauge in the range of 7 to 8 stitches per inch; and in worsted-weight yarn, you should still stay at 7 stitches per inch to be safe.

Here's another way to think of it. If you hold up your swatch to your eyes (you *will* swatch to check your gauge, right?) and you can see most of the person sitting across from you through the swatch, the fabric is probably tight enough for a decent pair of socks. If you can see the entire room in full detail, you've got some tightening up to do.

How you hold the yarn makes a big difference in terms of what guage you get. But two additional things impact gauge and the density of knitted fabric: the circumference of our knitting needle and the distance between the stitch we've just worked and the stitch we're about to work. The larger the circumference of our needle, the larger each loop is; the smaller the circumference, the smaller each loop. Larger loops tend to occupy more vertical space than smaller ones, meaning that we need fewer rows of stitches to fill each inch (or centimeter) of knitted fabric. If you want to increase your row and stitch gauge and create a more dense fabric for high-wear areas, such as heels and toes, drop down by one needle size. The change won't make too much of a visual difference, but it'll be a huge structural help.

While changing needle size may seem obvious, here's something less evident that I learned from Stephanie Pearl-McPhee: The farther apart we hold our needles (and the stitches *on* those needles), the farther apart each stitch will sit in the fabric. Which means that if we really want to tighten up our stitch gauge to make a firm, well-wearing sock, we simply need to pack our stitches as tightly as possible on the needles, and then hold those needles close together when knitting. Stranded colorwork requires a little more care so that the stitches don't pucker. But otherwise, trigger-loading our stitches is a simple and clever notion, and it works every time.

SLIPPING STITCHES

A discreet way to make your knitted fabric more snug is to slip a stitch, ideally at regular intervals between normally worked stitches. You can make the fabric extra dense by holding your yarn tight as you slip the stitch, which will also make your fabric pucker. Or, you can loosen the effect by keeping the yarn slack or even loose as you slip the stitch—losing a bit of the hug but maintaining more stretchiness in the process. We mostly use slipped stitches in sock heels, since they produce a double-thick cushion for comfort and reinforcement. But you can also use them in the leg and sole, as Ann Budd does in Annapurna (page 178), or in the footbed, as A. Karen Alfke does in Turbo Toes (page 173), to give even more cushion and strength to a sock.

Just keep in mind that fabric made from slipped stitches will be tighter than fabric made from plain stockinette and less elastic than ribbing.

STRANDING AND DOUBLE KNITTING

If slipped stitches don't give you the kind of thickness and strength you're looking for, here's another option: Simply knit your fabric from two strands of yarn, alternating one stitch from one strand and the next stitch from the other strand. This creates an extra-thick fabric with two layers of overlapping fiber that provide superior padding and strength. It's normally used for high-wear areas, such as heels, as you can see in my Stepping-Stones (page 56). You can also use stranded knitting all over when

Slipped stitches give cushion and strength to the footbed in A. Karen Alfke's Turbo Toes (page 173).

NYLON REINFORCEMENT: YES OR NO?

If you've read many sock patterns by now, you've probably seen one or two mentions of nylon reinforcing thread. It's often used alongside the working yarn to strengthen heel and toe stitches. I mentioned earlier that the crisscrossing fibers in twisted stitches may saw into one another when pressed and rubbed, snapping the fibers and causing a breach in your sock fabric. Priscilla Gibson-Roberts argues that the same thing happens when you strand nylon reinforcing thread along the stitches of your heel and toe. Elizabeth Zimmermann maintains that you only run this risk with thicker materials, such as fishing line.

It's primarily a blending issue. By virtue of not being evenly incorporated into the full surface area of the fabric, nylon reinforcing thread cannot offer as much complete support as would the same amount of nylon if intimately blended among all the other fibers. There's simply more nylon distributed throughout each stitch in an intimate blend than there is in a companion strand.

Still, many purists want to use as little synthetic fiber as possible—yet they acknowledge that their heels need a little boost. In addition to slipping stitches or knitting a double-thick heel, stranding some nylon can also help. Or, consider a sock yarn that has reinforcement from stronger natural fibers, such as mohair, silk, or mechanically processed bamboo. Though not as strong as nylon, they still offer some strengthening help.

When intimately blended among fibers in a sock yarn, nylon provides complete and integrated reinforcement to the fabric, as in Sandi Rosner's Hummingbird socks (page 137).

working with an innately more vulnerable yarn, which is what Jared Flood does with Strago (page 150). Or, for optimal plushness and reinforcement, consider knitting a true double-knit fabric like the one in Lucy Neatby's Cape Spear (page 154).

Stranded knitting does have its shortcomings, though. First, the fabric will be fairly tight and inelastic, which is why it's normally reserved for heels. And second—true for both stranded and double knitting—the fabric may be so thick that it won't fit comfortably into every shoe you own. Then again, with such comfortable padding on your feet, you may not want to wear any shoes at all.

HELPFUL HEELS

Not all heel techniques produce equally durable results. The standard flap-and-gusset heel gives great depth and bounce to all types of yarn, especially the less elastic ones. Short-row heels can look more sleek and tailored, but they tend to have less bounce because they're usually formed with simple stockinette. This same stockinette structure makes short-row heels more vulnerable to abrasion, especially if you tend to wear out the backs of your heels first. But if you tend to wear out the *bottoms* of your heels first, short-row heels have the advantage in that you can add nylon reinforcement that will span more of the bottom of the heel. Without any extra reinforcement, short-row heels are innately more vulnerable to abrasion. When working with patterns that incorporate this kind of heel, choose tighter-spun yarns that incorporate strong but elastic fibers. Knit a short-row heel from a gently spun singles and the sock won't survive its first wear—unless it's made from 100 percent nylon yarn, in which case *you* might not survive its first wear.

Short-row heels are also structurally shallower than the standard flap-and-gusset heel, which also makes them more vulnerable to wear. Lucy Neatby advises that you

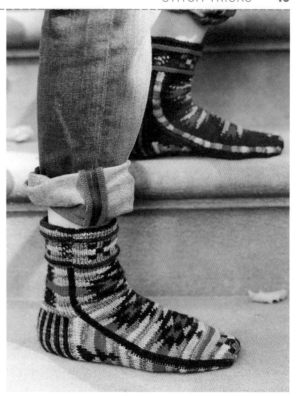

Double-knit fabric gives Lucy Neatby's Cape Spear socks (page 154) the ultimate cushioning.

use 60 percent of your total stitches for short-row heels instead of the standard flap-and-gusset heel formula in which you use 50 percent of your total stitches for the heel. Obviously, this becomes trickier if you're following a complicated pattern that requires all those stitches to stay where the designer wanted them to stay—but with a little creativity, anything is possible.

In either case, if you purl more loosely than you knit, Cat Bordhi recommends that you use a smaller needle to work the purl sides of heel rows to keep the fabric nice and dense. You could take the notion one step further and work the entire heel in a smaller needle for an even denser fabric.

A Final Note about Fit

When I first began knitting socks, they always turned out too long. I couldn't understand what was wrong because I always followed the patterns exactly as written. When they told me to begin toe decreases when the sock was 2 inches (5cm) from the desired length, that's exactly what I did.

I was confusing the desired sock length with my actual *foot* length. And the two are very, very different things. Socks need to fit snugly on your foot. Like a mattress pad, a well-fitting sock actually needs to be slightly smaller than the area it's intended to cover. Not tremendously smaller, but smaller nonetheless. This is called *negative ease*, and it's the most important and most overlooked requirement of a well-wearing sock.

Generally speaking, you'll want to maintain a negative ease of at least 10 percent in your sock, meaning that you'll want the sock to be 10 percent smaller than your foot—both in terms of leg circumference and overall sock length. At an absolute bare minimum, the sock should be ⅓ inch (8.5mm) shorter than your actual foot. You'll notice that the patterns in the next chapter all specify length in terms of the desired sock length and not the length of your foot. Please remember this distinction because it's important.

A well-wearing sock will hold snug to your foot, minimizing any slippage in the shoe, so that foot, sock, and shoe can move as one. If the sock is too large, it will slip on your foot and rub in your shoe. It will become misshapen and will wear out much faster—and you'll be grumpy and uncomfortable the whole time.

A well-wearing sock holds snug to your foot, with negative ease minimizing any slippage.

> *A well-wearing sock will hold **snug to your foot**, minimizing any slippage in the shoe, so that foot, sock, and shoe **can move as one.***

Feet and shoes make up the final magic piece of the sock puzzle. Socks are intended to protect our tender feet from the cold, sharp edges of the world, but they are not miracle workers. Rough nails and large calluses will gradually gnaw away at any tender fibers. And likewise, no matter how strong the fiber, how well-constructed the yarn, or how well-formed your stitches, an incompatible shoe can do great damage to socks in just a short time. Love your socks by putting them on well-tended feet and slipping them into well-fitting shoes, and your socks will love you back for many, many wearings to come.

Well-fitting shoes make up the final piece of the sock puzzle.

The Patterns

It's time to take out your needles and put sock theory to the test. The following twenty patterns were conceived to illustrate everything that can make a sock tick. To bring in as varied a perspective as possible, I asked nineteen bright and forward-thinking sock designers to lend their creative spirit to this book.

Conceptually, some of these sock patterns highlight the power of twist and elasticity, while others show the infinite variability of ribbing. Some demonstrate cables at their optimal three-dimensionality, while others showcase simple tricks for producing amazing padding and strength. You'll find patterns that thrive in solid colors or semisolids, and others designed expressly for variegated and self-patterning colorways. Patterns range in difficulty from easy to wow-this-isn't-as-hard-as-I-thought-it'd-be intermediate, with just a few meaty challenges to keep you on your toes. Each introduction explains why the pattern was conceived and what the designer and I hoped you'd learn from it.

SKILL LEVEL AND SPECIAL TECHNIQUES

You'll notice that the patterns do not include a skill level listing. According to the Craft Yarn Council's standard for skill levels, all of the socks in this book are either Intermediate or Experienced simply because they are knit in the round. I've met many a knitter whose very first project was a pair of socks, and I don't want any label to dissuade you from trying a pattern that appeals to you. Follow the pattern row by row, look up anything you don't yet know, and you can achieve any of the socks in this book. If you're just getting started and need a little extra hand-holding, consider Stepping-Stones (page 56) as your first project. This beginner top-down sock pattern includes a lot more explanatory information about what you're doing, and why you're doing it, at each stage of the sock's construction.

Any techniques that are unique to a particular pattern will be explained in the Stitch Guide within that pattern. Otherwise, you can find explanations for the other commonly used stitch terms in the Abbreviations and Techniques section beginning on page 187. In those cases where space did not permit a full technique tutorial, I point you to excellent online resources that will serve you well.

The patterns assume you already have a basic understanding of casting on, binding off, and working in the round. They are grouped by general technique and then by level of complexity within each technique. We begin with basic knit and purl stitch combinations, then cables and twisted stitches, lace and openwork, and finally colorwork.

The yarns specified in each pattern were chosen for a reason, but they are by no means the only yarns you can ever use. Each pattern introduction includes information about the qualities to seek when choosing a yarn, and it also includes total yardage requirements for easy substitutions. If you see a pattern call for *1–2 skeins* of a yarn, this means that we were able to complete one pair with the lower number, but there was very little yarn left over. If you tend to use more yarn than a pattern specifies, or if you know you'll be knitting a longer cuff or foot, go with the higher number just to be on the safe side. And, as always, I encourage you to be a free-range "yarnivore" and play with whatever yarn suits your personal fancy. Above all, have fun.

Stepping-Stones

Designed by Clara Parkes

Stepping-stones guide us from one place to the next. My hope is that these socks will start you on your own sock-knitting journey. If you're new to socks, or if you're feeling rusty and in need of a refresher course, begin here. Throughout the pattern you'll find lots of helpful hand-holding that will familiarize you with the fundamentals of sock construction.

This sock also serves as a gentle reminder that, while most so-called sock yarns are extremely fine, you can *knit a lovely pair of socks out of thicker yarns. For everyday comfort and wear, the maximum recommended thickness would be worsted-weight yarn, which is what I used in this pattern.*

Sock A (right) is knit using a springy and rounded three-ply Merino from Blue Moon Fiber Arts; and sock B (left) is knit using plush, though equally springy, four-ply Merino from Malabrigo. The pattern is simple enough to incorporate almost any color theme your heart desires, whether it be a solid or semisolid or, in the case of Malabrigo, a flickering multicolor.

SIZE
Women's M (Women's L/Men's M)

FINISHED MEASUREMENTS
Foot circumference: 7½ (7¾)" (19 [19.5]cm) unstretched, to fit foot circumference of about 8¾ (9.5)" (22 [23.5]cm)

YARN
300 (340) yd (274 [311]m) of worsted-weight yarn:
Sock A (right), in women's M: 1 skein Blue Moon Fiber Arts Socks That Rock Heavyweight, 100% superwash Merino, 7 oz (198g), 350 yd (320m), color Oregon Red Clover Honey
Sock B (left) in men's M: 2 skeins Malabrigo Rios, 100% superwash Merino, 3½ oz (100g), 210 yd (192m), color 862 Piedras

NEEDLES
Set of 4 U.S. size 2 (2.75mm) double-pointed needles, or size to obtain gauge

NOTIONS
Tapestry needle

GAUGE
28 stitches and 40 rows = 4" (10cm) in stockinette stitch (knit in the round)

Notes

▸ The heel flap is knit using two strands of yarn, working one stitch from one strand and the next stitch from the other strand, to create an extra-thick, plush, and durable heel. If you want to create a multicolored effect, you can use a contrasting color for the second strand. Otherwise, the easiest solution is to wind your yarn into a center-pull ball (using a ball winder, nostepinne, or your hands) and use the other end for the second strand.

▸ The Leg Pattern and Instep Pattern can be worked using either the charts provided or the written directions in the Stitch Guide.

▸ Slipped stitches are slipped as if to purl, with the yarn held to the wrong side of the work.

Stitch Guide

Leg Pattern

(Also see the Leg Chart on page 60.)

Round 1: *K1, p1; repeat from * to the end of the round.

Round 2: *K3, p3; repeat from * to the end of the round.

Instep Pattern

(Also see the Instep Chart on page 60.)

Round 1: (K1, p1) 3 times, (k5, p1) 3 times, (k1, p1) 2 times.

Round 2: K1, p3, k21, p3.

Cuff

Cast on 54 (60) stitches. Divide stitches evenly onto 3 needles. Join to work in the round, taking care not to twist the stitches.

Round 1: *K1, p1; repeat from * to the end of the round. Repeat this round until cuff measures 1½" (4cm).

Leg

Work in Leg Pattern on all stitches until the piece measures 6" (15cm) from the cast-on edge, or until desired leg length has been reached. End having worked round 2 of the pattern.

Heel Flap

Rearrange the stitches as follows: Place the first 26 (32) stitches on needle 1 for the heel, then divide the remaining 28 stitches over needles 2 and 3 and hold them aside to be worked later for the instep.

Using the working yarn and the other end of the same skein, work the heel back and forth in rows, alternating the 2 strands of yarn, as follows:

Row 1 (RS): Slip 1, (k1 with working yarn, k1 with second strand) 12 (15) times, k1 with the working yarn, turn work.

Row 2 (WS): Slip 1, (p1 with working yarn, p1 with second strand) 12 (15) times, p1 with the working yarn, turn.

Work rows 1 and 2 until the flap measures 2 (3)" (5 [7.5]cm); end having worked a wrong-side row. Cut the second strand of yarn and work the rest of the pattern with the original strand only.

Turn Heel

Row 1 (RS): Slip 1, k14 (18), ssk, k1. Turn work.

Row 2 (WS): Slip 1, p5 (7), p2tog, p1. Turn.

Row 3 (RS): Slip 1, knit to 1 stitch before the gap created by the turn on the previous row, ssk to close the gap (1 stitch from each side of the gap), k1. Turn.

Row 4 (WS): Slip 1, purl to 1 stitch before the gap created by the turn on the previous row, p2tog to close the gap (1 stitch from each side of the gap), p1. Turn. Repeat rows 3 and 4 until all stitches have been worked, ending with a wrong-side row—16 (20) heel stitches remain.

Gussets

Return to working in the round, as follows: With right side facing, slip 1, knit to the end of the heel needle. Then, using the same needle, pick up and knit 1 stitch in each selvedge stitch along the edge of the heel flap, and 1 stitch between the heel flap and the instep (this is now needle 1). With another needle, work round 1 of the Instep Pattern across the 28 instep stitches (this is now needle 2). With a third needle, pick up and knit 1 stitch between the instep and the heel flap and 1 stitch in each selvedge stitch along the edge of the heel flap, then knit across the first 8 (10) heel stitches (this is now needle 3). You are now ready to begin your instep decreases, which will happen on needles 1 and 3 every other round. Needle 2 will always be worked in the Instep Pattern.

Round 1: On needle 1, knit all stitches. On needle 2, work in the Instep Pattern as established. On needle 3, knit to the end of the round.

Round 2 (decrease): On needle 1, knit to the last 3 stitches, k2tog, k1. On needle 2, work in pattern as established. On needle 3, k1, ssk, knit to the end of the round.

Repeat rounds 1 and 2 until 28 (32) stitches remain on the sole (needles 1 and 3)—56 (60) stitches total.

Foot

Continue to work in the round, keeping to the established pattern on needle 2 and working in stockinette on needles 1 and 3 until the foot measures 1¾ (2)" (4.5 [5]cm) less than desired sock length. (For optimal fit and wear, the desired sock length should be at least 10 percent shorter than the actual foot length. See Foot Length Tables on page 191 for the actual foot length of common U.S. shoe sizes.)

Toe

For larger size only:

Toe setup: Slip the last stitch from needle 1 onto the beginning of needle 2. Slip the first stitch from needle 3 onto the end of needle 2—30 stitches on needle 2, 15 stitches each on needles 1 and 3.

For all sizes:

Round 1 (decrease): On needle 1, knit to the last 3 stitches, k2tog, k1. On needle 2, k1, ssk, knit to the last 3 stitches, k2tog, k1. On needle 3, k1, ssk, knit to the end of the round.

Round 2: Knit all stitches.

Repeat these 2 rounds until 20 total stitches remain, ending with round 1.

Knit across needle 1 and place those stitches on needle 3, then graft the toe closed with Kitchener stitch.

Weave in ends.

Repeat the pattern to make a matching pair.

Stepping-Stones Charts

Key
□ = K
⊡ = P

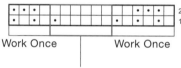

LEG CHART

6-Stitch Repeat

INSTEP CHART

Work Once   Work Once

Work 3 Times

Darjeeling

Designed by Cat Bordhi

This lovely sculptural creation uses purl rows and broken-rib elements to create bounce and form-fitting movement along the foot. The resulting fabric is strong yet stretchy both vertically and horizontally. And the arch expansion has been tucked along the bottom of the foot—a true Cat Bordhi touch.

For added durability, the sample sock was knit in an S-on-S cabled yarn whose roundedness also helps the purl stitches pop from the fabric. Semisolid and simple variegation enhance the feeling of horizontal movement along the foot, but you could also stick with a solid color to bring out the sculptural stitches in higher relief.

SIZE
Women's S (M, L)

FINISHED MEASUREMENTS
Foot circumference: 6¾ (7¼, 7¾)" (17 [18.5, 19.5]cm) unstretched, to fit foot circumference of about 7¾ (8¼, 8¾)" (19.5 [21, 22]cm)

YARN
310 (365, 420) yd (283 [334, 384]m) of fingering-weight yarn: 2 skeins Alchemy Juniper, 100% superfine Merino, 1¾ oz (50g), 232 yd (212m), color Grass Harp

NEEDLES
Sct of 5 U.S. size 1 (2.25mm) double-pointed needles, or size to obtain gauge

NOTIONS
Stitch markers
Tapestry needle

GAUGE
36 stitches and 53 rows = 4" (10cm) in stockinette stitch (knit in the round)

Notes

▸ *This pattern uses the modified version of Judy's Magic Cast-On, which does not twist the stitches on the second needle (see page 187). If you are using the original version of this cast-on, you will need to adjust your stitches accordingly.*

▸ *The Instep Pattern and Upper Leg Pattern can be worked using either the charts provided or the written directions in the Stitch Guide.*

▸ *See the Working Wrapped Stitches entry on page 190 for details about how to knit or purl a stitch together with its wrap.*

Stitch Guide

M1: Pick up the bar between the stitches from front to back, and knit into the back of the picked-up stitch.

M1P: Pick up the bar between the stitches from front to back, and purl into the back of the picked-up stitch.

Slip 1 tbl: With the yarn held to the wrong side of the work, insert the tip of the right-hand needle into the back loop of the next stitch on the left-hand needle as if to purl it through the back loop and slide the stitch to the right-hand needle without working it (twisting the stitch).

W&T (wrap and turn): With yarn to the wrong side of the work, slip the next stitch purlwise. Bring yarn to the right side of the work and move the slipped stitch back to the left-hand needle. Turn work, ready to knit or purl in the other direction.

Instep Pattern
(Also see the Instep Chart below.)
Round 1: Purl.
Rounds 2–4: K11 (12, 13), p4, k1, p4, k11 (12, 13).

Upper Leg Pattern
(Also see the Upper Leg Chart below.)
Round 1: Purl.
Rounds 2–3: P4, k1, p4, k2, (p2, k2) 13 (14, 15) times.
Round 4: P4, k1, p4, knit to the end of the round.

Darjeeling Charts

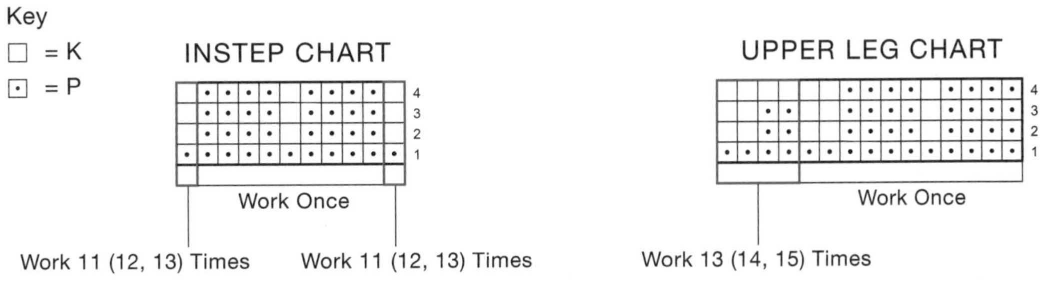

Key
□ = K
⊡ = P

INSTEP CHART

Work Once

Work 11 (12, 13) Times   Work 11 (12, 13) Times

UPPER LEG CHART

Work Once

Work 13 (14, 15) Times

Toe

Using Judy's Magic Cast-On (see page 187), cast on 11 stitches onto 2 parallel needles—22 stitches total. Knit 11 stitches (across 1 needle).

Round 1: *K1, M1, k9, M1, k1; repeat from * once—26 stitches total.

Round 2: Knit.

Round 3: *K2, M1, place marker, k9, place marker, M1, k2; repeat from * once—30 stitches total.

Round 4: Knit.

Round 5: *Knit to marker, M1, slip marker, k9, slip marker, M1; repeat from * once. Knit to the end of the round—34 stitches total.

Repeat the last 2 rounds until you have 62 (66, 70) stitches total. Knit 3 rounds, removing markers.

Foot

The first set of 31 (33, 35) stitches is the instep; the second set of 31 (33, 35) stitches is the sole. Use needle intersections or markers to separate these sets of stitches.

Work the Instep Pattern over the instep stitches, and knit all the stitches on the sole. Continue as established until work measures 4½ (4¾, 5)" (11.5 [12, 12.5]cm) less than desired sock length.

Arch Expansion

Round 1: Maintain pattern as established on the instep. On the sole, K15 (16, 17), place marker, M1, k1, M1, place marker, knit to the end of the round—64 (68, 72) stitches total.

Rounds 2–3: Maintain pattern as established on the instep, knit all stitches on the sole.

Round 4: Maintain pattern as established on the instep. On the sole, knit to marker, slip marker, M1, k to marker, M1, slip marker, k to the end of the round.

Repeat rounds 2–4 until there are 31 (33, 35) stitches between the markers on the sole—92 (98, 104) stitches total.

Turn Heel

Work pattern as established to the end of the instep stitches, then hold these stitches aside to be worked later. Work the heel back and forth in rows on sole stitches only, as follows:

Row 1 (RS): Knit to the first marker on the sole, slip marker, knit to 2 stitches before the second marker, W&T.

Row 2 (WS): Purl to 2 stitches before the marker, W&T.

Row 3 (RS): Knit to 3 stitches before the marker, W&T.

Row 4 (WS): Purl to 3 stitches before the marker, W&T.

Row 5 (RS): Knit to 4 stitches before the marker, W&T.

Row 6 (WS): Purl to 4 stitches before the marker, W&T.

Continue in this manner, wrapping and turning 1 additional stitch before each marker until 7 (8, 9) sequential stitches have been wrapped on each side with 15 unwrapped stitches at the center.

Next row (RS): K15, knit each of the next 6 (7, 8) stitches together with their wraps, lift the wrap on the next stitch and knit the next 2 stitches together with the lifted wrap, remove marker, turn—91 (97, 103) stitches total.

Next row (WS): Slip 1 purlwise with yarn to the wrong side of the work, p 21 (22, 23), purl each of the next 6 (7, 8) stitches together with their wraps, lift the wrap on the next stitch and purl the next 2 stitches together with the lifted wrap, remove marker, turn—90 (96, 102) stitches total.

Back of Heel

Continue to work back and forth in rows over the sole stitches as follows:

Row 1 (RS): Slip 1 tbl, (ktbl, k1) 13 (14, 15) times, ktbl, ssk, turn.

Row 2 (WS): Slip 1 tbl, p1, (ptbl, p1) 13 (14, 15) times, p2tog, turn.

Repeat the last 2 rounds until only 2 stitches remain unworked on each end of the heel; end having worked a wrong-side row.

Next row (RS): Slip 1 tbl, (ktbl, k1) 13 (14, 15) times, ktbl, ssk, k1. Do not turn.

Leg

With right side facing, resume working in the round, as follows: Work across the instep stitches in the Instep Pattern as established. Then knit the first heel stitch, k2tog, knit to the end of the heel stitches. Place marker to indicate a new end of round—62 (66, 70) stitches total, with 31 (33, 35) stitches on the instep/front of leg and 31 (33, 35) stitches on the heel/back of leg.

Round 1: On instep stitches, maintain the Instep Pattern as established. On heel/back of leg stitches, (p1, k1) 15 (16, 17) times, p1.

Repeat the last round until ribbing at the back of the leg measures about 2" (5cm) high, and a round 4 of the Instep Pattern has been completed.

Upper Leg

Remove end-of-round marker. M1P, p11 (12, 13), place marker to indicate a new end of round—63 (67, 71) stitches total.

Work the Upper Leg Pattern on all stitches until the leg measures about 5" (12.5cm) from the bottom of the ribbing, ending with pattern round 1. Purl 1 round.

Bind off very loosely using a traditional bind-off or Jeny's Surprisingly Stretchy Bind-Off (see page 187). Weave in ends.

Repeat the pattern to make a matching pair.

Hickory

Designed by Jane Cochran

Like broad brushstrokes on a canvas, we can group our stitches together to create larger motifs in our knitting—which is what Jane Cochran did here. The discreet staggering of increases and decreases within a slender purl column creates a gently undulating, barklike ribbing that is both visually appealing and functionally strong and stretchy.

To enhance the sense of depth and movement, the sample was knit in a springy two-ply Sundara Sock Yarn, which gives a hint of shadow to the fabric. The flickering semisolid coloring further enhances the sense of movement. You could also knit these socks out of a solid color or even a semisolid that incorporates two complementary colors. But be wary of any greater variegation, which could overpower and detract from the subtle beauty of the stitch pattern.

SIZE
Women's M

FINISHED MEASUREMENTS
Foot circumference: 6½" (16.5cm) unstretched, to fit foot circumference of about 8¼" (21cm)

YARN
360 yd (330m) of fingering-weight yarn: 1–2 skeins Sundara Yarn Sock Yarn, 100% superwash Merino wool, 3½ oz (100g), 370 yd (338m), color Ruby Most Sought After

NEEDLES
Set of 5 U.S. size 1 (2.25mm) double-pointed needles, or size to obtain gauge

NOTIONS
Stitch markers
Tapestry needle

GAUGE
36 stitches and 49 rows = 4" (10cm) in stockinette stitch (knit in the round)

Notes

▶ *The Leg Pattern and the Instep Pattern can be worked using either the charts provided or the written directions in the Stitch Guide.*

▶ *Slipped stitches are slipped as if to purl, with the yarn held to the wrong side of the work.*

Stitch Guide

M1PR (make 1 purl stitch right): With the tip of the left needle, pick up the bar between stitches from back to front. Purl the picked-up stitch through the front loop.

Leg Pattern

(Also see the Leg Chart opposite.)

Round 1: *K3, M1PR, k3, p2tog; repeat from * to the end of the round.

Rounds 2–8: *K3, p1; repeat from * to the end of the round.

Round 9: *K3, p1, M1PR, k2, ssk; repeat from * to the end of the round.

Rounds 10–16: *K3, p2, k3; repeat from * to the end of the round.

Round 17: *K3, p2tog, k3, M1PR; repeat from * to the end of the round.

Rounds 18–24: *K3, p1; repeat from * to the end of the round.

Round 25: *K2, ssk, k3, p1, M1PR; repeat from * to the end of the round.

Rounds 26–32: *K6, p2; repeat from * to the end of the round.

Instep Pattern

(Also see the Instep Chart opposite.)

Setup round (work only once): P2tog, *k3, M1PR, k3, p2tog; repeat from * 3 times—33 stitches.

Rounds 1–7: P1, *k3, p1; repeat from * 7 times.

Round 8: K2tog, k2, p1, M1PR, k2, ssk, *k3, p1, M1PR, k2, ssk; repeat from * 2 times—32 stitches.

Rounds 9–15: *K3, p2, k3; repeat from * 3 times.

Round 16: M1PR, *k3, p2tog, k3, M1PR; repeat from * 3 times—33 stitches.

Rounds 17–23: P1, *k3, p1; repeat from * 7 times.

Round 24: P1, *k2, ssk, k3, p1, M1PR; repeat from * 2 times, k2, ssk, k3, p1—32 stitches.

Rounds 25–31: P1, *k6, p2; repeat from * 2 times, k6, p1.

Round 32: P1, *k3, M1PR, k3, p2tog; repeat from * 2 times, k3, M1PR, k3, p1—33 stitches.

Repeat rounds 1–32 for pattern.

Cuff

Loosely cast on 64 stitches, and divide them evenly onto 4 double-pointed needles. Join to work in the round, being careful not to twist the stitches around the needles. Place marker to indicate the end of the round.

Round 1: *K2, p2; repeat from * to the end of the round. Repeat this round until the piece measures about 1" (2.5cm) from the cast-on edge.

Leg

Work in the Leg Pattern on all stitches. Complete 2 full repeats of the pattern, or as many complete repeats as needed to reach the desired leg length. End having worked round 32 of the pattern.

Hickory Charts

Key

☐ = K

⊡ = P

◪ = K2tog

◪ = SSK

◬ = P2tog

◪ = Pick up bar between sts from back to front and purl the picked-up stitch

▩ = No Stitch

INSTEP CHART

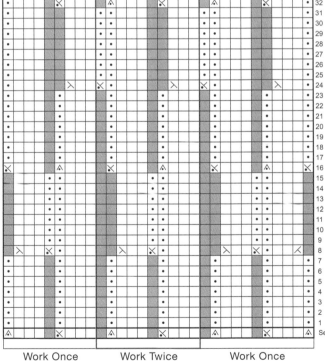

Work Once   Work Twice   Work Once

LEG CHART

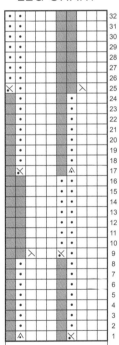

8-Stitch Repeat

Heel Flap

Remove marker and arrange the first 30 stitches on needle 1 for the heel. Arrange the remaining 34 stitches on needles 2 and 3 and hold aside to be worked later for the instep.

The heel flap is worked back and forth in rows on needle 1, as follows:

Row 1 (RS): *Slip 1, k1; repeat from * to the end of the heel needle. Turn work.

Row 2 (WS): Slip 1, purl to the end of the needle, turn.

Repeat these 2 rows until a total of 32 rows have been worked, or until the heel flap is the desired length. End having worked a wrong-side row.

Turn Heel

Row 1 (RS): Slip 1, k16, ssk, k1, turn.

Row 2 (WS): Slip 1, p5, p2tog, p1, turn.

Row 3: Slip 1, knit to 1 stitch before the gap formed by the turn on the previous row, ssk (using 1 stitch on each side of the gap), k1, turn.

Row 4: Slip 1, purl to 1 stitch before the gap formed by the turn on the previous row, p2tog (using 1 stitch on each side of the gap), p1, turn.

Repeat rows 3 and 4 until all stitches have been worked, ending with a wrong-side row—18 heel stitches remain.

Gussets

With right side facing, resume working in the round as follows: On needle 1, knit across the 18 heel stitches, pick up and knit 16 stitches along the edge of the heel flap, pick up and knit 1 more stitch in the space between the heel flap and the instep. On needles 2 and 3, work in the Instep Pattern (beginning with the setup round) over the held-aside instep stitches. Using a fourth needle, pick up and knit 1 stitch in the space between the instep and the heel flap, pick up and knit 16 stitches along the other edge of the heel flap, knit 9 heel stitches from needle 1. Place marker to indicate a new end of round.

Round 1: On needle 1, knit to the last 3 stitches, k2tog, k1. On needles 2 and 3, continue to work the Instep Pattern as established. On needle 4, k1, ssk, knit to the end of the round.

Round 2: On needle 1, knit all stitches. On needles 2 and 3, work in pattern as established. On needle 4, knit to the end of the round.

Repeat the last 2 rounds until 32 stitches remain on the sole (needles 1 and 4).

Note: As you work the Instep Pattern on needles 2 and 3, the number of stitches on the instep will vary depending on which round of the stitch pattern you are working.

Foot

Continue to work in stockinette stitch on needles 1 and 4 and in the Instep Pattern on needles 2 and 3 until the foot measures 1¾" (4.5cm) less than the desired sock length. End after completing any one of any of the following rounds of the Instep Pattern: 1–7, 16–23, or 32. 65 stitches total (33 on the instep, 32 on the sole).

Toe

Remove marker, knit to the end of needle 1, place marker to indicate a new end of round.

Round 1: K2tog, k2, p1, (k3, p1) 6 times, k4, place marker, knit to the end of the round—64 stitches total (32 on the instep, 32 on the sole).

Round 2: K1, ssk, p1, (k3, p1) to 4 stitches before the marker, k1, k2tog, k1, slip marker, k1, ssk, knit to 3 stitches before the end of the round, k2tog, k1.

Round 3: K2, p1, (k3, p1) to 3 stitches before the marker, k3, slip marker, knit to the end of the round.

Round 4: K1, ssk, work in k3, p1 rib as established (knitting the knits and purling the purls) to 3 stitches before the marker, k2tog, k1, slip marker, k1, ssk, knit to 3 stitches before the end of the round, k2tog, k1.

Round 5: K2, work in k3, p1 rib as established (knitting the knits and purling the purls) to 2 stitches before the marker, k2, slip marker, knit to the end of the round.

Repeat the last 2 rounds 2 more times—48 stitches remain.

Round 10: *K1, ssk, knit to 3 stitches before the marker, k2tog, k1, slip marker; repeat from * once.

Round 11: Knit all stitches.

Repeat the last 2 rounds 2 more times, then repeat round 10 only 5 times—16 stitches remain.

Move all instep stitches to one needle and all sole stitches to another needle. Graft toe closed with Kitchener stitch.

Weave in ends.

Repeat the pattern to make a matching pair.

Elm

Designed by Cookie A

A master of the broad brushstroke, Cookie A uses the clever pairing of increases and decreases within a simple rib motif to create the illusion of smooth, overlapping branches. While the pattern has less elasticity than a straightforward k2/ p2 ribbing, there's still sufficient stretch for a comfortable fit.

To enhance those broad brushstrokes of stitches even further, she knit the socks in a smooth, well-rounded, three-ply yarn whose dusting of cashmere softens the high-relief effect of the stitches. You could still work these socks in a springy two-ply Merino, such as Louet Gems; just know that the yarn's ply shadows will tone down the brightness of the stitch motif.

Semisolid coloring gives a third dimension of depth to the stitch pattern, but it would look equally lovely in a solid color. Avoid using yarns that have too much color variation, however, as that would quickly overpower the stitch pattern.

SIZE
Women's M

FINISHED MEASUREMENTS
Foot circumference: 7" (18cm) unstretched, to fit foot circumference of about 8½" (21.5cm)

YARN
400 yd (366m) of fingering-weight yarn: 1–2 skeins String Theory Caper Sock, 80% Merino, 10% cashmere, 10% nylon, 4 oz (114g), 400 yd (366m), color Light Teal

SUPER FINE

NEEDLES
Set of 4 U.S. size 1 (2.25mm) double-pointed needles, or size to obtain gauge

NOTIONS
3 stitch markers
Tapestry needle

GAUGE
33 stitches and 50 rows = 4" (10cm) in stockinette stitch (knit in the round)

Notes

▸ *Slipped stitches are slipped as if to purl, with the yarn held to the wrong side of the work.*

Stitch Guide

M1: Pick up the bar between the stitches from front to back, and knit into the back of the picked-up stitch.

Cuff

Cast on 60 stitches and distribute so that each needle has a multiple of 12 stitches. Join to work in the round, being careful not to twist the stitches around the needles. Place marker to indicate the beginning of the round.

Round 1: *P3, k3; repeat from * to the end of the round. Repeat this round until the piece measures about 1½" (4cm) from the cast-on edge.

Leg

Work Chart A (opposite) over all stitches.

When all rounds of the chart have been completed, shift the beginning of the round 9 stitches to the right, as follows: Remove marker, k6, (p3, k9) 3 times, p3, k6, ending 9 stitches before the end of the previous round, place marker to indicate a new beginning of round. Redistribute the stitches so that each needle again has a multiple of 12 stitches.

Work Chart B (opposite) over all stitches.

When all rounds of the chart have been completed, shift the beginning of the round 9 stitches to the left, as follows: Remove marker, k3, p3, k3, place marker to indicate new beginning of round. Redistribute stitches so that each needle again has a multiple of 12 stitches. Work all rounds of Chart C (page 76), then work all rounds of Chart A.

When both charts have been completed, shift the beginning of the round 9 stitches to the right, as follows: Remove marker, k6, (p3, k9) 3 times, p3, k6, ending 9 stitches before the end of the previous round, place marker to indicate a new beginning of round. Redistribute stitches so that each needle again has a multiple of 12 stitches.

Work rounds 1–9 of Chart B.

Heel Flap

Rearrange stitches, as follows: Remove marker, k3, p3. Arrange the next 33 stitches on 2 needles and hold them aside to be worked later for the instep. Move the remaining 27 stitches (6 stitches just worked plus 21 stitches from the end of the previous round) to 1 needle to be worked for the heel.

Turn the work so that the wrong side is facing. The heel flap is worked back and forth in rows, as follows:

Row 1 (WS): Slip 1, p26, turn.

Row 2 (RS): (Slip 1, k1) 13 times, k1, turn.

Repeat these 2 rows until the heel flap measures 2½" (6.5cm); end having worked a wrong-side row.

Turn Heel

Row 1 (RS): Slip 1, k15, ssk, k1, turn.

Row 2 (WS): Slip 1, p6, p2tog, p1, turn.

Row 3 (RS): Slip 1, knit to 1 stitch before the gap formed by the turn on the previous row, ssk (using 1 stitch on each side of the gap), k1, turn.

Row 4 (WS): Slip 1, purl to 1 stitch before the gap formed by the turn on the previous row, p2tog (using 1 stitch on each side of the gap), p1, turn.

Repeat rows 3 and 4 until all heel stitches have been worked, ending with a wrong-side row—17 heel stitches remain.

Gussets

Resume working in the round as follows: Slip 1, k8, place marker to indicate a new beginning of round. Knit the remaining heel stitches, pick up and knit 1 stitch in each slipped stitch along the edge of the heel flap, M1, knit the first held stitch, place marker to indicate the right side of the instep, work Chart D (page 76) across the next 31 held stitches, place marker to indicate the left side of the instep, knit the last held stitch, M1, pick up and knit 1 stitch in each slipped stitch along the edge of the heel flap, knit to the end of the round.

Round 1: Knit to 2 stitches before marker (the right side of the instep), k2tog, slip marker, work Chart D to the next marker (the left side of the instep), slip marker, ssk, knit to the end of the round.

Round 2: Knit to the marker, work Chart D to the next marker, knit to the end of the round.

Repeat the last 2 rounds until 62 stitches remain—31 stitches on the instep and 31 stitches on the sole.

Foot

Continue working sole stitches in stockinette and instep stitches (between markers) according to Chart D, until the foot measures 1¾" (4.5cm) less than the desired sock length from the back of the heel turn.

Toe

Remove the end-of-round marker, knit to the marker at the right side of the instep. This is the new beginning of round.

Round 1: Knit to the end of the round.

Round 2: K1, ssk, knit to 3 stitches before the marker at the left side of the instep, k2tog, k1, slip marker, k1, ssk, knit to 3 stitches before the end of the round, k2tog, k1.

Repeat the last 2 rounds until 22 total stitches remain. Arrange the instep stitches on one needle and the sole stitches on another needle, then graft the toe closed with Kitchener stitch.

Weave in ends.

Repeat the pattern to make a matching pair.

Elm Chart

Key

☐ = K

· = P

⟋ = K2tog

⟍ = SSK

= Pick up bar between sts from front to back, k into back of picked-up st

= Pick up bar between sts from back to front, k into front of picked-up st

= Pick up bar between sts from front to back, p into back of picked-up st

= Pick up bar between sts from back to front, p into front of picked-up st

CHART A

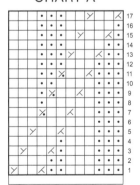

12-Stitch Repeat

Elm Charts

Key

☐ = K

· = P

⊠ = K2tog

⊠ = SSK

⊠ = Pick up bar between sts from front to back, k into back of picked-up st

⊠ = Pick up bar between sts from back to front, k into front of picked-up st

⊠ = Pick up bar between sts from front to back, p into back of picked-up st

⊠ = Pick up bar between sts from back to front, p into front of picked-up st

CHART D

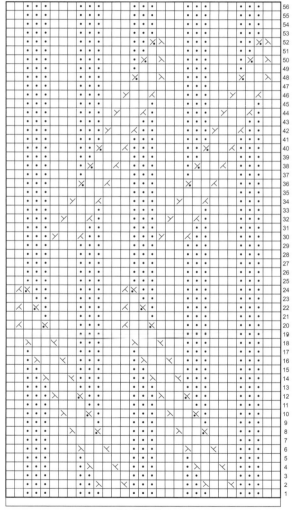

31 Stitches

CHART B

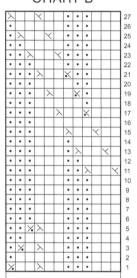

12-Stitch Repeat

CHART C

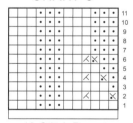

12-Stitch Repeat

Salted Caramels

Designed by Stephen Houghton

With its subtle texture set against a smooth stockinette background, this men's ribbed sock is simple and complex at the same time—rather like the flavor of salted caramels. The well-rounded, four-ply Zitron Trekking Pro Natura you see here renders the quietly nuanced faux cables with great clarity, while the mechanically processed bamboo adds welcome reinforcement and a discreet but not overbearing hint of sheen.

Columns of ribbing divide each textured section, adding welcome elasticity to balance out the tight increases and decreases Stephen uses within the stitch pattern. As a judicious design touch, two columns of ribbing continue uninterrupted along the length of the heel.

SIZE
Men's M (L)

FINISHED MEASUREMENTS
Foot circumference: 8 (8¾)" (20.5 [22]cm) unstretched, to fit foot circumference of about 10 (11)" (25.5 [28]cm)

YARN
570 (675) yd (521 [617]m) of fingering-weight yarn: 2 (2) skeins Zitron Trekking Pro Natura. 75% superwash wool, 25% unprocessed bamboo, 3½ oz (100g), 459 yd (420m), color 1503 Mocha

NEEDLES
2 U.S. size 0 (2.0mm) 16" (40cm) circular needles, or size to obtain gauge
An extra 2 circular needles (any length) of same size or smaller than those used to obtain gauge

NOTIONS
Tapestry needle
Stitch markers

GAUGE
36 stitches and 49 rows = 4" (10cm) in stockinette stitch (knit in the round)

Notes

▸ *These socks are worked on two circular needles. When working in the round on two circular needles, use only one needle at a time. Let both ends of the resting needle hang down out of the way while you work with the other needle. Each needle is used to work only the stitches on that needle.*

▸ *These socks begin with a provisional cast-on (page 189) that serves as the base of the hemmed cuff. The inside face of the cuff is worked first, followed by a purled turning round, and then the outside face of the cuff. The two faces are joined by knitting each stitch of the outside face together with a stitch from the provisional cast-on at the base of the inside face.*

▸ *The extra set of needles is used for holding the stitches that are released from the provisional cast-on and then joined with the working stitches to form the hem.*

▸ *Slipped stitches are slipped as if to purl, with yarn held to the wrong side of the work.*

▸ *The gussets for these socks are placed on the sides of the sole, rather than on the sides of the instep.*

▸ *The Salted Caramels Pattern can be worked using either the chart provided or the written directions in the Stitch Guide.*

Stitch Guide

Kfb: Knit through the front loop of the next stitch but do not take it off the left-hand needle; knit through the back loop of the same stitch, then slip both stitches off the left-hand needle.

Rli (right lifted increase): Insert the tip of the right needle from front to back into the right leg of the stitch below the next stitch on the left needle. Raise this stitch onto the left needle and knit it.

Lli (left lifted increase): Insert the tip of the left needle from front to back into the left leg of the stitch that is 2 stitches below the stitch you just worked on the right needle. Raise this stitch onto the left needle and knit it.

Salted Caramels Pattern

(Also see the Salted Caramels Chart on page 83.)

Round 1: *K2, k2tog, k1, rli, k2, lli, k1, ssk, k2, p2 (3); repeat from * to the end of the round.

Round 2: *K12, p2 (3); repeat from * to the end of the round.

Round 3: *K1, k2tog, k1, rli, k4, lli, k1, ssk, k1, p2 (3); repeat from * to the end of the round.

Round 4: As round 2.

Round 5: *K2tog, k1, rli, k6, lli, k1, ssk, p2 (3); repeat from * to the end of the round.

Rounds 6–7: As round 2.

Round 8: *K1, lli, k1, ssk, k4, k2tog, k1, rli, k1, p2 (3); repeat from * to the end of the round.

Round 9: As round 2.

Round 10: *K2, lli, k1, ssk, k2, k2tog, k1, rli, k2, p2 (3); repeat from * to the end of the round.

Round 11: As round 2.

Round 12: *K3, lli, k1, ssk, k2tog, k1, rli, k3, p2 (3); repeat from * to the end of the round.

Round 13–14: As round 2.

Rounds 15–17: As rounds 1–3.

Rounds 18–19: As round 2.

Rounds 20–24: As rounds 10–14.

Round 25: As round 1.

Rounds 26–27: As round 2.

Rounds 28–40: As rounds 12–24.

Cuff

Using a provisional cast-on method, cast on 78 (84) stitches. Divide stitches evenly onto 2 circular needles. Join to work in the round, taking care not to twist the stitches.

Rounds 1–12: Knit all stitches.

Round 13: Purl.

Rounds 14–25: Knit.

Join the hem, as follows: Remove the provisional cast-on and slide the 78 (84) released stitches onto 2 empty circular needles, placing half of the stitches on each needle. Fold the work in half along the purl turning row so that wrong sides are together and the released stitches are inside the working stitches. Join the 2 sides of the hem by knitting together each stitch on the outside needle with the corresponding stitch on the inside needle.

Leg

Round 1: *K12, kfb, p0 (1); repeat from * 5 times—84 (90) stitches.

Round 2: *K12, p2 (3); repeat from * 5 times.

Work in Salted Caramels Pattern on all stitches.

Complete 2 full repeats of the pattern, then work rounds 1–14 again.

Heel Flap

Arrange the next 40 (42) stitches onto 1 needle for the heel flap. The remaining 44 (48) stitches will be held aside on the other needle to be worked later as the instep. The heel flap is worked back and forth in rows on the heel needle, as follows:

Row 1 (RS): *(Slip 1, k1) 6 times, p2 (3); repeat from * 1 time, (slip 1, k1) 6 times. Turn work.

Row 2 (WS): Slip 1, p11, *k1, slip 1, k0 (1), p12; repeat from * 1 time. Turn.

Repeat last 2 rows 23 (29) more times.

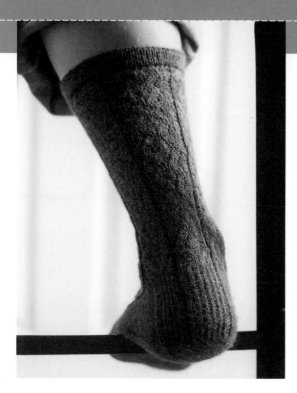

Turn Heel

Row 1 (RS): Slip 1, k24 (26), ssk, k1, turn.

Row 2 (WS): Slip 1, p11 (13), p2tog, p1, turn.

Row 3 (RS): Slip 1, knit to 1 stitch before gap formed by the turn on the previous row, ssk (using 1 stitch on each side of the gap), k1, turn.

Row 4 (WS): Slip 1, purl to 1 stitch before the gap formed by the turn on the previous row, p2tog (using 1 stitch on each side of the gap), p1, turn.

Repeat the last 2 rows until all stitches have been worked, ending with a wrong-side row—26 (28) heel stitches remain.

Gussets

Return to working in the round, as follows: Knit 26 (28) stitches across the heel. Continuing with the heel needle, pick up and knit 24 (30) stitches along the edge of the heel flap. With the instep needle, purl the first 2 (3) instep stitches, then work the remaining instep stitches in Salted Caramels Pattern as established (resuming with round 15 of the pattern). With the heel needle, pick up and knit 24 (30) stitches along the other edge of the heel flap, knit 13 (14) heel stitches. Place marker to indicate a new end of round—118 (136) stitches.

Round 1: K37 (44), purl the first 2 (3) stitches on the instep, work the remaining instep stitches in the Salted Caramels Pattern as established, k37 (44).

Round 2: K14, place marker, ssk, k21 (28), purl the first 2 (3) stitches on the instep, work the remaining instep stitches in the Salted Caramels Pattern as established, k21 (28), k2tog, place marker, k14—116 (134) stitches.

Round 3: Knit to the end of the heel needle, work the instep as established, knit to the end of the round.

Round 4: As round 3.

Round 5: Knit to the marker, slip marker, ssk, knit to the end of the heel needle, work the instep as established, knit to 2 stitches before the next marker, k2tog, slip marker, knit to the end of the round.

Repeat rounds 3–5 until 62 (66) stitches remain on the sole needle.

Then repeat rounds 4–5 until 40 (44) stitches remain on the sole needle—84 (92) stitches total.

Toe

Setup round: K20 (22), ssk, k12 (13), ssk, k12 (14), k2tog, k12 (13), k2tog, k20 (22)—80 (88) stitches, with an equal number of stitches on the instep and the sole needles.

Round 1: Knit all stitches.

Round 2: Knit to the last 4 stitches on the sole needle, k2tog, k2. On the instep needle, k2, ssk, knit to last 4 stitches on needle, k2tog, k2. On the heel needle, k2, ssk, knit to the end of the round.

Repeat these 2 rounds 9 (11) more times—40 stitches remain.

Work round 2 only 3 times—28 stitches remain.

Knit to the end of the sole needle. Graft the toe closed with Kitchener stitch.

Weave in ends.

Repeat the pattern to make a matching pair.

Foot

Continue to work in the round, keeping to the established pattern on the instep needle and working in stockinette stitch on the sole needle, until the foot measures about 2 (2½)" (5 [6.5]cm) less than the desired sock length. (For the best appearance, stop working the pattern on the instep after completing any one of the following pattern rounds: 7, 14, 19, 24, 30, 35, or 40. Then continue in stockinette until the specified length has been reached.)

Salted Caramels Chart

Key

☐ = K

· = P

☒ = K2tog

☒ = SSK

☒ = Insert tip of left needle from front to back into left leg of the st that is 2 sts below the st you just worked on right needle. Raise this stitch onto left needle and knit it.

☒ = Insert tip of right needle from front to back into right leg of the st below the next st on left needle. Raise this stitch onto left needle and knit it.

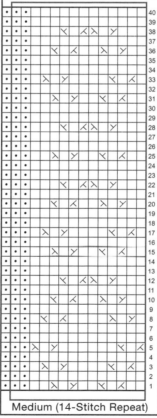

Medium (14-Stitch Repeat)

Large (15-Stitch Repeat)

Firefly

Designed by Jennifer Hagan

Cables can come in all shapes and sizes. Here Jennifer discreetly placed them within four-stitch columns of smooth stockinette separated by single columns of purl stitches. With fewer purl stitches to offset the cables, they recede more quietly into the background—while that single purl column still keeps the cuff comfortably stretchy.

The simplicity of the overall motif makes this pattern suitable for solid and semisolid colorways. Here the socks are shown in a hand-dyed, three-ply wool yarn with a healthy dose of nylon reinforcement. Remember that the rounder the yarn, the smoother and clearer the stitch pattern will be; the more textured the yarn, the more toned-down the pattern. You can also tone it down even further by choosing a yarn that has a dusting of a down undercoat fiber, such as cashmere, bison, or yak.

SIZE
Women's M

FINISHED MEASUREMENTS
Foot circumference: 6¾" (17cm) unstretched, to fit foot circumference of about 8½" (21.5cm)

YARN
300 yd (274m) of fingering-weight yarn: 1 skein Lorna's Laces Shepherd Sock, 80% superwash wool, 20% nylon, 3.5 oz (100g), 435 yd (398m), color Bold Red

NEEDLES
Set of 4 U.S. size 1 (2.25mm) double-pointed needles, or size to obtain gauge

NOTIONS
Cable needle
Stitch marker
Tapestry needle

GAUGE
32 stitches and 45 rows = 4" (10cm) in stockinette stitch (knit in the round)

Notes

▸ *Slipped stitches are slipped as if to purl, with the yarn held to the wrong side of the work.*

▸ *The Firefly Cable Pattern can be worked using either the chart provided or the written directions in the Stitch Guide.*

Stitch Guide

2/2RC (2-over-2 right-cross cable): Slip 2 stitches onto the cable needle and hold in the back of the work, k2 from the left-hand needle, k2 from the cable needle.

2/2RC dec (2-over-2 right-cross cable decrease): Slip 2 stitches to the cable needle and hold in the back of the work, k2tog (eliminating a purl stitch), k1, k2 from the cable needle.

Firefly Cable Pattern

(Also see the Firefly Cable Chart opposite.)

Rounds 1–3: *K4, p1; repeat from * to the end of the round.

Round 4: *2/2RC, p1, K4, p1; repeat from * to the end of the round.

Rounds 5–11: As round 1.

Round 12: *K4, p1, 2/2RC, p1; repeat from * to the end of the round.

Rounds 13–15: As round 1.

Round 16: As round 12.

Rounds 17–23: As round 1.

Round 24: As round 4.

Cuff

Cast on 72 stitches, dividing the stitches evenly among 3 double-pointed needles. Join to work in the round, being careful not to twist the stitches around the needles. Place marker to indicate the beginning of the round.

Rounds 1–12: *K2, p1; repeat from * to the end of the round.

Leg

Gradually decrease to set up for leg pattern, as follows:

Round 1: *(K2, p1) twice, 2/2RC dec, p1; repeat from * to the end of the round—66 stitches total.

Rounds 2–4: *(K2, p1) twice, k4, p1; repeat from * to the end of the round.

Round 5: *(K2, p1) twice, 2/2RC, p1; repeat from * to the end of the round.

Rounds 6–12: As round 2.

Round 13: *2/2RC dec, p1, k4, p1; repeat from * to the end of the round—60 stitches total.

Begin working in the Firefly Cable Pattern on the remaining 60 stitches. Continue in pattern until the piece measures 6" (15cm) from the cast-on edge, or until the desired leg length has been reached. End having worked any pattern round *except* 12–16. Do not work the last 3 stitches of the last round; just slip them purlwise onto the right-hand needle. Make a note of the last pattern round worked.

Heel Flap

Remove marker and rearrange the stitches as follows: Place the last 3 (unworked) stitches of the previous round and the first 27 stitches of the next round onto needle 1 for the heel. Divide the remaining 30 stitches over needles 2 and 3 and hold them aside to be worked later for the instep.

Work back and forth in rows on needle 1 only, as follows:

Row 1 (RS): K2, *slip 1, k1; repeat from * to the last 2 stitches on the needle, k2, turn.

Firefly Cable Chart

Key

☐ = K

⊡ = P

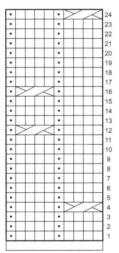 = Slip 2 sts to cable needle and hold in back, k2, k2 from cable needle

10-Stitch Repeat

Row 2 (WS): K2, purl to the last 2 stitches on the needle, k2, turn.

Repeat these 2 rows 13 more times—28 rows on the heel flap.

Turn Heel

Row 1 (RS): K17, ssk, k1, turn.

Row 2 (WS): Slip 1, p5, p2tog, p1, turn.

Row 3 (RS): Slip 1, knit to 1 stitch before the gap formed by the turn on the previous row, ssk (using 1 stitch on each side of the gap), k1, turn.

Row 4 (WS): Slip 1, purl to 1 stitch before the gap formed by the turn on the previous row, p2tog (using 1 stitch on each side of the gap), p1, turn.

Repeat the last 2 rows until all heel stitches have been worked, ending with a wrong-side row—18 heel stitches remain.

Gussets

With right side facing, resume working in the round as follows: Using an empty needle, knit across the 18 heel stitches, then pick up and knit 14 stitches along edge of the heel flap. (Pick up stitches from the running thread between the purl "bumps" on the garter-stitch edge of the heel flap, and knit them through the back loop to tighten them slightly.) Pick up and knit 1 more stitch in the corner between the heel flap and the instep. Using a second needle, knit the first 2 instep stitches, p1, work the next 25 instep stitches in the Firefly Cable Pattern as established (this will be 2½ repeats of the pattern), k2. Using a third needle, pick up and knit 1 stitch in the corner between the instep and the heel flap, pick up and knit 14 stitches along the edge of the heel flap, then knit 9 heel stitches—78 stitches total (24 on needle 1, 30 on needle 2, and 24 on needle 3). Place marker to indicate a new beginning of round.

Round 1: On needle 1, knit to the last 3 stitches, k2tog, k1. On needle 2, k2, p1, work in the Firefly Cable Pattern as established to the last 2 stitches, k2. On needle 3, k1, ssk, knit to the end of the round.

Round 2: On needle 1, knit all stitches. On needle 2, k2, p1, work in the Firefly Cable Pattern as established to the last 2 stitches, k2. On needle 3, knit to the end of the round.

Repeat these 2 rounds until needles 1 and 3 each have 15 stitches remaining—60 stitches total.

Foot

Continue working the sole stitches (needles 1 and 3) in stockinette stitch and the instep stitches (needle 2) in pattern as established until the foot measures 1½" (4cm) less than the desired sock length from the back of the heel turn.

Toe

Round 1: On needle 1, knit to the last 3 stitches, k2tog, k1. On needle 2, k1, ssk, work in the Firefly Cable Pattern as established to the last 3 stitches, k2tog, k1. On needle 3, k1, ssk, knit to the end of the round.

Round 2: On needle 1, knit. On needle 2, k2, work in pattern as established to the last 2 stitches, k2. On needle 3, knit.

Repeat these 2 rounds (carrying the cable pattern as far down the toe as the decreasing stitch count will allow) until 24 total stitches remain.

Knit across needle 1, and graft the toe closed with Kitchener stitch.

Weave in ends.

Repeat the pattern to make a matching pair.

Rocaille

Designed by Norah Gaughan

Norah Gaughan speaks in cables the way I speak English—only better. This pattern was conceived to showcase the well-rounded, three-dimensional qualities of a true cable-spun or S-on-S cabled yarn. It renders Norah's cables in an exquisite high relief that evokes the elegant, shell-inspired scroll ornamentation in Rococo design, called rocaille. An abundance of reverse stockinette stitch pushes the cables even further away from the fabric surface, while also putting the fabric's soft, smooth stockinette side against your skin.

With its multiple stacked ribs along the front, the orientation of the cable motif does add elasticity to enhance the reverse-stockinette fabric. But if you have larger calves and suspect that elasticity will be an issue, consider using a four-ply or S-on-S cabled yarn whose dominant fibers have plenty of built-in elasticity.

SIZE
Women's M

FINISHED MEASUREMENTS
Foot circumference: 7¼" (18.5cm) unstretched, to fit foot circumference of about 8¼" (21cm)

YARN
390 yd (357m) of fingering-weight yarn: 1 skein Berroco Comfort Sock, 50% superfine nylon, 50% superfine acrylic, 3½ oz (100g), 447 yd (412m), color 1713 Dusk

NEEDLES
Set of 5 U.S. size 3 (3.25mm) double-pointed needles, or size to obtain gauge
Set of 5 U.S. size 1 (2.25mm) double-pointed needles, or 2 sizes smaller than needles used to obtain gauge

NOTIONS
Stitch markers
1–2 yards of fingering-weight scrap yarn, preferably in a contrasting color
Cable needle
Tapestry needle

GAUGE
30 stitches and 40 rows = 4" (10cm) in stockinette stitch on larger needles (knit in the round)

Cuff

With smaller needles, cast on 68 stitches. Join to work in the round, being careful not to twist the stitches around the needles. Place marker to indicate the beginning of the round.

Round 1: *K1, p2, k1; repeat from * to the end of the round.

Repeat the last round until the work measures 2" (5cm) from the cast-on edge.

Leg

Change to larger needles and work the Leg Chart (page 93) through round 80—60 stitches remain.

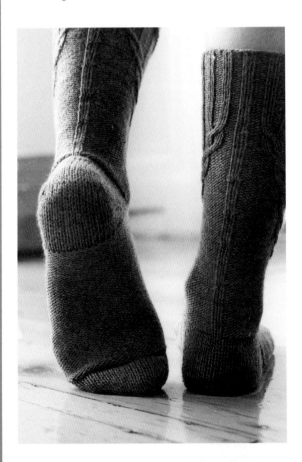

Heel Opening

Make an opening for the heel by working back and forth in rows, as follows:

Row 1 (RS): K1, p26, k2, p2, k2, p12. Drop the working yarn but do not cut it. Thread a tapestry needle with a length of scrap yarn and slide the next 15 stitches onto the scrap yarn, remove the end-of-round marker, and slide the next 15 stitches onto the scrap yarn. Hold these 30 stitches aside to be worked later for the afterthought heel (which is added, as the term "afterthought" suggests, after you've completed the rest of the sock). The 30 stitches remaining on the needles are the instep stitches. Return to where the working yarn was dropped. Turn the work to the wrong side.

Row 2 (WS): Pick up the working yarn and k12, p2, k2, p2, k12. Turn the work.

Row 3 (RS): P12, k2, p2, k2, p12. Drop the working yarn, but do not cut it. Do not turn.

Using a piece of fingering-weight scrap yarn in a contrasting color and an empty double-pointed needle in the larger size, cast on 30 stitches for the sole. Cut the scrap yarn. Pick up the dropped working yarn and purl across the first 15 cast-on stitches, place end-of-round marker, purl the remaining 15 cast-on stitches. Join back into a round by working across the instep stitches as follows: P8, place marker 1, p4, k2, p2, k2, p4, place marker 2, p8. Then purl the first 15 sole stitches, and place another marker to indicate the end of the round—60 stitches total.

Foot

Round 1: Purl to marker 1, slip marker, work the Foot Chart (page 92) to marker 2, slip marker, purl to the end of the round.

Repeat the last round until the Foot Chart is complete. Remove markers 1 and 2, leaving only the end-of-round marker.

Rocaille Charts

Key

☐ = K

⊡ = P

⊠ = K2tog

⊠ = SSK

⊙ = YO

■ = No Stitch

▱⊠▱ = Slip 2 sts to cable needle and hold in front, k2, k2 from cable needle

▱⊠⊡ = Slip 2 sts to cable needle and hold in front, p2, k2 from cable needle

▱⊠▱ = Slip 2 sts to cable needle and hold in back, k2, k2 from cable needle

⊡⊠▱ = Slip 2 sts to cable needle and hold in back, k2, p2 from cable needle

▱⊠▱ = Slip 4 sts to cable needle and hold in back, k2, slip last 2 sts from cable
needle to left-hand needle and p2, k2 from cable needle

FOOT CHART

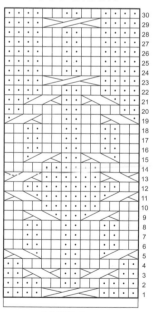

14 Stitches

LEG CHART

68 Stitches

Next round: P27, k2, p2, k2, p27.

Repeat the last round until the sole measures 3½" (9cm) less than the desired length of the sock from the heel opening.

Toe

Place markers after the fifteenth and the forty-fifth stitches. Then work the toe, as follows. (Note that the toe decreases are worked opposite the usual way.)

Round 1: Knit all stitches.

Round 2: *Knit to 3 stitches before the marker, ssk, k1, slip marker, k1, k2tog; repeat from * once. Knit to the end of the round.

Round 3: Knit.

Repeat rounds 1–3 two more times, repeat rounds 2–3 three times, then repeat round 2 twice—28 stitches remain.

Knit to the first marker. Place the next 14 stitches on one needle and the remaining 14 stitches on another needle and graft the toe closed with Kitchener stitch.

Afterthought Heel

Carefully remove the scrap yarn cast-on from the sole stitches. Place the 30 released stitches on 2 of the larger-size needles. Place the 30 back-of-leg stitches held on the scrap yarn onto another 2 larger-size needles.

Next round: With sock yarn, pick up 3 stitches in the gap between the 30 leg stitches and the 30 sole stitches at one side of the heel. Knit across the 30 sole stitches. Pick up 3 stitches in the gap at the other side of the heel. Knit across the 30 leg stitches, knit the first 2 picked-up stitches, place end-of-round marker—66 total stitches. Place another marker after the thirty-third stitch.

Round 1: *K1, k2tog, knit to 3 stitches before the next marker, ssk, k1, slip marker; repeat from * once.

Round 2: Knit.

Round 3: Knit.

Repeat rounds 1–3 once more, repeat rounds 1–2 four times, then repeat round 1 three times—30 stitches remain.

Place the next 15 stitches on one needle and the remaining 15 stitches on another needle and graft the heel closed with Kitchener stitch.

Weave in ends.

Repeat the pattern to make a matching pair.

Buddleia

Designed by Marlaina Bird

Down fibers are extremely soft, lightweight, and insulating. They're perfect for socks, until you remember that they tend to be the shortest and most vulnerable of all protein fibers. But need that stop you? Not if you can find a yarn that blends these fibers with a good amount of nylon (in this case, 15 percent nylon has been added to 85 percent yak) and gives sufficient twist to hold the fibers together.

Because yak and other down fibers tend to be quite warm, I asked Marlaina to open up the fabric with natural "vents" created through lace yarn-overs. She also included a few purl columns along the cuff and top of the foot to preserve elasticity.

The yarn's two-ply structure keeps the cables relatively close to the fabric surface, but you could easily brighten up these socks by knitting them in a smooth three- or four-ply yarn. A solid or a gentle semisolid colorway will best complement the latticelike stitch pattern. Any more variegation will conceal all your lovely stitchwork.

SIZE
Women's M (L)

FINISHED MEASUREMENTS
Foot circumference: 8 (9)" (20.5 [23]cm) unstretched, to fit foot circumference of about 8½ (9½)" (21.5 [24]cm)

YARN
260 (320) yd (238 [293]m) of fingering-weight yarn: 1 skein Bijou Basin Ranch Bijou Spun Tibetan Dream Sock Yarn, 85% pure yak, 15% nylon, 4 oz (113g), 440 yd (402m), color Natural Cream

NEEDLES
2 U.S. size 1 (2.25mm) 16" (40cm) circular needles, or size to obtain gauge

NOTIONS
Cable needle
Stitch markers
Tapestry needle

GAUGE
32 stitches and 48 rows = 4" (10cm) in stockinette stitch (knit in the round)

Notes

▸ *This pattern uses the modified version of Judy's Magic Cast-On, which does not twist the stitches on the second needle (see page 187). If you are using the original version of this cast-on, you will need to adjust your stitches accordingly.*

▸ *These socks are worked on two circular needles. When working in the round on two circular needles, use only one needle at a time. Let both ends of the resting needle hang down out of the way while you work with the other needle. Each needle is used to work only the stitches on that needle.*

▸ *The Cable Pattern and the Lace Pattern can be worked using either the charts provided or the written directions in the Stitch Guide.*

▸ *The sock is shown in size Large, which has alternating cable and lace panels around the leg. In size Medium, there is no lace panel separating the cables along either side.*

▸ *See the Working Wrapped Stitches entry on page 190 for details about how to knit a stitch together with its wrap.*

Stitch Guide

M1: Pick up the bar between the stitches from front to back, and knit into the back of the picked-up stitch.

C4b: Slip 2 stitches onto the cable needle and hold in the back of the work, k2 from the left-hand needle, k2 from the cable needle.

C4f: Slip 2 stitches onto the cable needle and hold in the front of the work, k2 from the left-hand needle, k2 from the cable needle.

Kfb: Knit through the front loop of the next stitch but don't take it off the left-hand needle; knit through the back loop of the same stitch, then slip both stitches off the left-hand needle.

Pfb: Purl through the front loop of the next stitch but don't take it off the left-hand needle; purl through the back loop of the same stitch, then slip both stitches off the left-hand needle.

W&T (wrap and turn): With yarn to the wrong side of the work, slip the next stitch purlwise. Bring yarn to the right side of the work and move the slipped stitch back to the left-hand needle. Turn work, ready to knit or purl in the other direction.

Cable Pattern

(Also see the Cable Chart on page 99.)

Rounds 1–2: P1, k6, p1.

Round 3: P1, k2, c4f, p1.

Rounds 4–6: P1, k6, p1.

Round 7: P1, c4b, k2, p1.

Round 8: P1, k6, p1.

Lace Pattern

(Also see the Lace Chart on page 99.)

Round 1: P1, k1, (k2tog) twice, (yo, k1) 3 times, yo, (ssk) twice, k3, p1.

Round 2 (and all even-numbered rounds): P1, k15, p1.

Round 3: P1, (k2tog) twice, yo, k1, yo, k3, yo, k1, yo, (ssk) twice, k2, p1.

Round 5: P1, k3, (k2tog) twice, (yo, k1) 3 times, yo, (ssk) twice, k1, p1.

Round 7: P1, k2, (k2tog) twice, yo, k1, yo, k3, yo, k1, yo, (ssk) twice, p1.

Round 8: As round 2.

Toe

Using Judy's Magic Cast-On (see page 187) and 2 circular needles, cast on 15 (17) stitches onto each needle—30 (34) stitches total.

Round 1: Knit all stitches.

Round 2: On needle 1, k1, M1, knit to the last stitch on the needle, M1, k1. Repeat for needle 2.

Repeat the last 2 rounds until there are 33 (37) stitches on each needle—66 (74) stitches total.

Foot

Round 1: On needle 1 (instep), p0 (2), work round 1 of the Cable Pattern, round 1 of the Lace Pattern, round 1 of the Cable Pattern, p0 (2). On needle 2 (sole), knit all stitches.

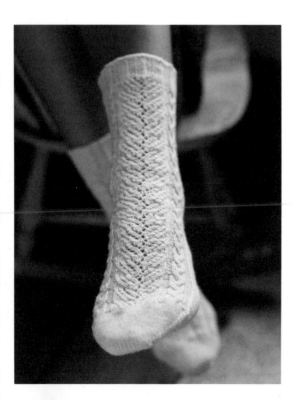

Continue working in pattern on the instep needle and in stockinette on the sole needle until the piece measures 2½" (2¾") (6.5 [7]cm) less than the desired sock length.

Gussets

Round 1: On needle 1, work in pattern as established. On needle 2, k1, M1, knit to the last stitch on the needle, M1, k1.

Round 2: On needle 1, work in established pattern. On needle 2, knit.

Repeat the last 2 rounds until there are 55 (61) stitches on needle 2—88 (98) stitches total.

Heel Turn

Work in pattern across the stitches on needle 1 (instep). Then work back and forth in rows on needle 2 (the sole) only, as follows:

Row 1 (RS): K37 (41), kfb, k1, W&T.
Row 2 (WS): P22 (24), pfb, p1, W&T.
Row 3 (RS): K20 (22), kfb, k1, W&T.
Row 4 (WS): P18 (20), pfb, p1, W&T.
Row 5 (RS): K16 (18), kfb, k1, W&T.
Row 6 (WS): P14 (16), pfb, p1, W&T.
Row 7 (RS): K12 (14), kfb, k1, W&T.
Row 8 (WS): P10 (12), pfb, p1, W&T.
Needle 2 now has 63 (69) stitches.

Back of Heel

Knit to the end of needle 2, knitting each wrap together with the stitch it wraps. Then work across needle 1 in established pattern.

Resume working back and forth in rows on needle 2 only, as follows:

Row 1 (RS): K47 (52), knitting each remaining wrap together with the stitch it wraps, ssk, turn.
Row 2 (WS): Slip 1 knitwise, p31 (35), p2tog, turn.

Row 3 (RS): (Slip 1 knitwise, k1) 16 (18) times, ssk, turn.

Repeat rows 2–3 until all stitches on needle 2 have been worked; end having completed a row 2.

Next row (RS): Knit across needle 2, increasing 0 (1) stitch on this row—33 (38) stitches on needle 2—66 (75) stitches total.

Leg

Return to working in the round, as follows:

Medium Size Only

Round 1: On needle 1 (front of leg), work in established pattern. On needle 2 (back of leg), work in the same pattern as on needle 1, following the same pattern row.

Large Size Only

Rearrange the stitches on the needles as follows: Purl the first 2 stitches of needle 1 onto needle 2, then move the last 2 stitches of needle 1 onto needle 2—33 stitches on needle 1, 42 stitches on needle 2.

Round 1: On needle 1 (front of leg), work in established pattern (but without the extra 2 purl stitches on each end of the needle). On needle 2 (back of leg), work the same row of the Lace Pattern as on needle 1, the same row of the Cable Pattern, and then the same row of the Lace Pattern once more. The leg now consists of 3 repeats of the Cable Pattern and 3 repeats of the Lace Pattern in an alternating sequence.

Both Sizes

Work in pattern as established until the piece measures about 1½" (4cm) less than the desired leg length.

Cuff

Round 1: *(P1, k2, p1) 2 times, (p2, k3) 3 times, p2, (p1, k2, p1) 2 (0) times; repeat from * to the end of the round.

Repeat the last round until the cuff measures 1½" (4cm) or the desired length.

Bind off using Elizabeth Zimmermann's Sewn Bind-Off (see page 187).

Weave in ends.

Repeat the pattern to make a matching pair.

Buddleia Charts

Key

☐ = K

⊡ = P

◸ = K2tog

◹ = SSK

⊙ = YO

 = Slip 2 sts to cable needle and hold in front, k2, k2 from cable needle

= Slip 2 sts to cable needle and hold in back, k2, k2 from cable needle

CABLE CHART

8 Stitches

LACE CHART

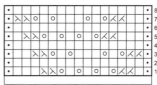

17 Stitches

Veil of Rosebuds

Designed by Anne Hanson

Silk is a gorgeous fiber—lustrous, soft, and strong. But elastic it is not. As soon as Anne started swatching with the 70 percent Merino, 30 percent silk blend shown in Version A (opposite), she realized that the fabric was much more dense and firm than it would be with a 100 percent Merino. She shifted to a lace pattern with meandering stockinette and areas of open mesh created with stretchy yarn-overs, k2togs, and ssks. The mesh was designed to open up the fabric and improve its elasticity.

Knit in a 100 percent wool yarn (as in Version B, page 102), you'll immediately notice a jump in stretch, though the sock will lose density and luster in the process. In terms of colors, gentle variegation enhances the movement within the stitch pattern, although more than two contrasting colors in the variegation might prove overpowering.

Both versions are made from a two-ply yarn that gives flickering ply shadows to the fabric. Move to a rounder yarn, or a more loosely plied yarn with a softer surface, and the patterning will smooth out considerably.

SIZE
Women's S (M, L)

FINISHED MEASUREMENTS
Foot circumference: 5¼ (7, 8¾)" (13.5 [18, 22] cm) unstretched, to fit foot circumference of about 7 (8½, 10)" (18 [21.5, 25.5]cm) in circumference

YARN
300 (350, 425) yd (274 [320, 389]m) of fingering-weight yarn:
Sock A (left): 1 (1, 2) skeins A Verb for Keeping Warm Metamorphosis, 70% superwash Merino, 30% silk, 4 oz (114g), 385 yd (352m), color The Peacock's Wild Plume
Sock B (page 102): 1 (1, 2) skeins Madelinetosh

Tosh Sock, 100% superwash Merino, 4 oz (110g), 395 yd (361m), color Celadon

NEEDLES
Set of U.S. 4 size 1 (2.25 mm) double-pointed needles, or size to obtain gauge

NOTIONS
Tapestry needle

GAUGE
30 stitches and 40 rows = 4" (10cm) in stockinette stitch (knit in the round)

Notes

▸ *The Leg and Instep Patterns can be worked using either the charts provided or the written directions in the Stitch Guide.*

▸ *See the Working Wrapped Stitches entry on page 190 for details about how to knit or purl a stitch together with its wrap.*

Stitch Guide

W&T knitwise (wrap and turn knitwise): Move yarn between the needles to the front, slip the next stitch purlwise, move yarn between the needles to the back, move the slipped stitch back to the left-hand needle, and turn the work.

W&T purlwise (wrap and turn purlwise): Move yarn between the needles to the back, slip the next stitch purlwise, move yarn between the needles to the front, move the slipped stitch back to the left-hand needle, and turn the work.

Leg Pattern

(Also see the Leg Chart on page 106.)

Rounds 1 and 7: *(Yo, ssk) 3 times, p1, yo, k2, ssk, k2, p1; repeat from * to the end of the round.

Round 2 (and all even-numbered rounds): *K6, p1; repeat from * to the end of the round.

Rounds 3 and 9: *(Yo, ssk) 3 times, p1, k1, yo, k2, ssk, k1, p1; repeat from * to the end of the round.

Rounds 5 and 11: *(Yo, ssk) 3 times, p1, k2, yo, k2, ssk, p1; repeat from * to the end of the round.

Rounds 13 and 19: *K2, k2tog, k2, yo, p1, (k2tog, yo) 3 times, p1; repeat from * to the end of the round.

Rounds 15 and 21: *K1, k2tog, k2, yo, k1, p1, (k2tog, yo) 3 times, p1; repeat from * to the end of the round.

Rounds 17 and 23: *K2tog, k2, yo, k2, p1, (k2tog, yo) 3 times, p1; repeat from * to the end of the round.

Round 24: As round 2.

Instep Pattern

(Also see the Instep Chart on page 106.)

Rounds 1 and 7: (P1, yo, k2, ssk, k2) 1 (0, 1) times, *p1, (yo, ssk) 3 times, p1, yo, k2, ssk, k2; repeat from * 0 (1, 1) times, p1.

Round 2 (and all even-numbered rounds): (P1, k6) 3 (4, 5) times, p1.

Rounds 3 and 9: (P1, k1, yo, k2, ssk, k1) 1 (0, 1) times, *p1, (yo, ssk) 3 times, p1, k1, yo, k2, ssk, k1; repeat from * 0 (1, 1) times, p1.

Rounds 5 and 11: (P1, k2, yo, k2, ssk) 1 (0, 1) times, *p1, (yo, ssk) 3 times, p1, k2, yo, k2, ssk; repeat from * 0 (1, 1) times, p1.

Rounds 13 and 19: (P1, [k2tog, yo] 3 times) 1 (0, 1) times, *p1, k2, k2tog, k2, yo, p1, (k2tog, yo) 3 times; repeat from * 0 (1, 1) times, p1.

Rounds 15 and 21: (P1, [k2tog, yo] 3 times) 1 (0, 1) times, *p1, k1, k2tog, k2, yo, k1, p1, (k2tog, yo) 3 times; repeat from * 0 (1, 1) times, p1.

Rounds 17 and 23: (P1, [k2tog, yo] 3 times) 1 (0, 1) times, *p1, k2tog, k2, yo, k2, p1, (k2tog, yo) 3 times; repeat from * 0 (1, 1) times, p1.

Round 24: As round 2.

Cuff

Cast on 42 (56, 70) stitches over 2 double-pointed needles held together (or use another elastic cast-on method). Divide stitches onto 3 needles in multiples of 2. Join to work in the round, taking care not to twist the stitches around the needles.

Round 1: *K1, p1; repeat from * to the end of the round. Repeat this round until the cuff measures 1½ (1½, 2)" (4 [4, 5]cm) from the cast-on edge.

Leg

Divide stitches so that there is a multiple of 14 stitches on each needle. Work in the Leg Pattern on all stitches. Complete 2 (3, 3) full repeats of the pattern, or as many complete repeats as needed to reach the desired leg length. End having worked round 24 of the pattern.

Heel

Rearrange the stitches as follows: Place the first 20 (27, 34) stitches on needle 1 for the heel. Then divide the remaining 22 (29, 36) stitches over needles 2 and 3 and hold aside to be worked later for the instep.

The heel is worked back and forth in rows over the stitches on needle 1, as follows:

Row 1 (RS): Knit to 1 stitch before the end of needle 1, W&T knitwise.

Row 2 (WS): Purl to 1 stitch before the end of the needle, W&T purlwise.

Row 3 (RS): Knit to the last unwrapped stitch (leaving it unworked), W&T knitwise.

Row 4 (WS): Purl to the last unwrapped stitch (leaving it unworked), W&T purlwise.

Repeat rows 3 and 4 until there are 8 (9, 10) stitches left unwrapped at the center of the heel, ending with a wrong-side row.

Row 1 (RS): Knit across the unwrapped stitches, then pick up the wrap of the next stitch and knit it together with that stitch. Then W&T knitwise so that the next stitch has 2 wraps on it.

Row 2 (WS): Purl across the unwrapped stitches, then pick up the wrap of the next stitch and purl it together with that stitch. Then W&T purlwise so that the next stitch has 2 wraps on it.

Row 3 (RS): Knit to the double-wrapped stitch, pick up both wraps and knit them together with that stitch, then W&T knitwise.

Row 4 (WS): Purl to the double-wrapped stitch, pick up both wraps and purl them together with that stitch, then W&T purlwise.

Repeat rows 3 and 4 until all single-wrapped stitches have been worked, ending with a wrong-side row. At this point, there is one double-wrapped stitch at each end of needle 1.

Next row (RS): Knit to 1 stitch before the end of needle 1, pick up both wraps on that stitch and knit them together with the stitch. Do not turn. The double-wrapped stitch at the other end of the needle will be worked on the next round.

Foot

Rearrange the stitches as follows: Divide the heel stitches between needles 1 and 3, and place all the patterned instep stitches onto needle 2. The working yarn will be at the end of needle 1, ready to work the first patterned instep stitch.

Work across needle 2 in the Instep Pattern, beginning with round 1 of the pattern. Begin needle 3 by picking up the wraps that remain around the first stitch and knitting them together with that stitch, then knit to the end of needle 3. From this point, rounds will begin and end here, at the center of the heel—42 (56, 70) total stitches.

Continue to work the foot in rounds, keeping to the established pattern on needle 2 and working in stockinette on needles 1 and 3. When the sock *nears* the desired foot length minus 1 (1½, 2)" (2.5 [4, 5]cm), end the stitch pattern with the nearest round 12 or 24 (the remaining length to the start of the toe will be worked in stockinette as described below).

Next round: Knit around, decreasing 1 stitch on needle 2 and increasing 1 stitch on needle 3—42 (56, 70) stitches total, with an equal number of stitches on the instep (needle 2) and the sole (needles 1 and 3). Continue in stockinette on all needles until the sock measures the correct length to begin toe shaping— desired foot length minus 1 (1½, 2)" (2.5 [4, 5]cm).

Toe

Round 1: On needle 1, knit to the last 3 stitches, k2tog, k1. On needle 2, k1, ssk, knit to the last 3 stitches, k2tog, k1. On needle 3, k1, ssk, knit to the end of the round.

Round 2: Knit all stitches.

Repeat these 2 rounds until 22 (24, 26) total stitches remain, ending with round 1.

Knit across needle 1 and place those stitches on needle 3, then graft the toe closed with Kitchener stitch.

Weave in ends.

Repeat the pattern to make a matching pair.

Veil of Rosebuds Charts

Key

☐ = K

⊡ = P

⊠ = K2tog

⊠ = SSK

⊡ = YO

LEG CHART

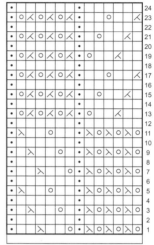

14-Stitch Repeat

INSTEP CHART

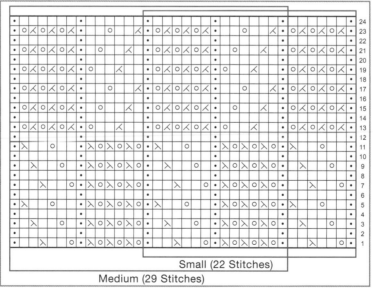

Small (22 Stitches)

Medium (29 Stitches)

Large (36 Stitches)

Isabella d'Este

Designed by Jayme Stahl

Lace needn't be a fragile affair. In honor of this sock's inherent beauty and underlying strength, I named it after Isabella d'Este, one of the strongest and most influential women of the Renaissance period.

While lace is typically knit in two-ply yarns, Jayme fortified this lace-inspired design with a stronger, rounder three-ply yarn that blends Merino, silk, and cashmere. Staggered openwork rosettes culminate in an elegant teardrop diamond at the top of the foot, while the surrounding stockinette gives the smoothest fit and most comfortable wear. Alternating slipped stitches in the heel gives welcome reinforcement, and a picot-edged cuff hides k1/p1 ribbing for much needed elasticity. In fact, the lack of any significant ribbing dictates that you use a yarn with a high percentage of elastic fibers.

Knit in a subtly variegated hand-dyed yarn, the sock takes on a gently weathered patina. Avoid any strongly contrasting variegation, whose horizontal jabs of color would interrupt the downward flow of the pattern.

SIZE
Women's S (M, L)

FINISHED MEASUREMENTS
Foot circumference: 7½ (8½, 9½)" (19 [21.5, 24]cm) unstretched

YARN
270 (335, 415) yd (247 [306, 379]m) of heavy fingering-weight yarn: 1 (1, 2) skeins Spirit Trail Fiberworks Sunna, 75% superwash Merino, 15% cashmere, 10% bombyx silk, 4 oz (110g), 350 yd (320m), color Apricot Flambeau

NEEDLES
Set of 5 U.S. size 1 (2.25mm) double-pointed needles, or size to obtain gauge
Extra set of needles of the same size or smaller than those used to obtain gauge

NOTIONS
Stitch markers
Tapestry needle

GAUGE
32 stitches and 40 rows = 4" (10cm) in stockinette stitch (knit in the round)

Notes

▸ *This sock has a hemmed picot edge. The instructions explain how to form the hem while knitting, using an extra set of needles. Alternatively, the hem can be sewn down after all knitting is complete. To do this you will need to leave an extra-long tail from your cast-on, omit the row 12 setup, and simply knit row 12 in stockinette.*

▸ *To adjust the length of the leg of the sock, knit fewer or more repeats of Chart A before moving on to Chart B. However, be sure to end Chart A with the round specified for the size sock you are making.*

▸ *The gusset decreases for these socks occur on the instep within the charted lace pattern.*

▸ *Slipped stitches are slipped as if to purl, with the yarn held to the wrong side of the work.*

Cuff

Loosely cast on 60 (68, 76) stitches and divide them onto 4 needles so that needles 1 and 4 each have 14 (18, 18) stitches and needles 2 and 3 each have 16 (16, 20) stitches. Join to work in the round, being careful not to twist the stitches around the needles.

Rounds 1–5: *K1, p1; repeat from * to the end of the round.

Round 6 (picot/folding round): *Yo, p2tog; repeat from * to the end of the round.

Rounds 7–11: Knit all stitches.

Setup for round 12: With the extra needles, pick up (but do not knit) 30 (34, 38) stitches from the cast-on edge (pick up 1 stitch from every other cast-on stitch). Fold the cuff in half along the picot/folding round so the wrong sides are together, the picked-up stitches are to the inside of the cuff, and the working stitches are to the outside.

Round 12: *Knit 1 outside stitch, knit 1 outside stitch together with 1 inside stitch (k2tog); repeat from * to the end of the round—60 (68, 76) total stitches.

Leg

Work Chart A (page 112) over all the stitches. Complete 2 full repeats of the pattern, then work rounds 1–8 once more.

Work Chart B (page 112) over all the stitches. Continue in pattern until all rounds of the chart are complete.

Work Chart C (page 113) over all the stitches, repeating the central portion (red-outlined box) of the chart 4 (5, 6) times around. Continue as established until rounds 1–8 of the chart are complete.

Next round: K4, work Chart C (repeating the central portion of the chart 3 [4, 5] times around), k4. Repeat the last round until rounds 1–8 of the chart are complete.

Next round: K8, work Chart C (repeating the central portion of the chart 2 [3, 4] times around), k8. Repeat the last round until rounds 1–8 of the chart are complete.

Next round: K12, work Chart C (repeating the central portion of the chart 1 [2, 3] times around), k12. Continue as established until rounds 1–4 (8, 8) of the chart are complete.

Large Size Only

Next round: K16, work Chart C (repeating the central portion of the chart 2 times around), k16. Continue as established until rounds 1–4 of the chart are complete.

Heel Flap

Rearrange stitches as follows: Move the last 15 (17, 19) stitches of the round onto an empty needle, then knit the first 16 (18, 20) stitches of the round onto the same needle to be worked for the heel. Place the next 29 (33, 37) stitches on 2 needles and hold aside to be worked later for the instep.

Turn the work so the wrong side is facing. The heel is worked back and forth in rows, as follows:

Row 1 (WS): Slip 1, purl to the end of the needle. Turn work.

Row 2 (RS): *Slip 1, k1; repeat from * to the last stitch on the needle, k1, turn.

Row 3 (WS): Slip 1, purl to the end of the needle, turn.

Row 4 (RS): Slip 1, k2, *slip 1, k1; repeat from * to the last 2 stitches on the needle, k2, turn.

Continue working these 4 rows until there are 31 (37, 43) total rows on the heel flap; end having completed a wrong-side row.

Turn Heel

Row 1 (RS): Slip 1, k17 (19, 21), ssk, k1. Turn work.

Row 2 (WS): Slip 1, p6, p2tog, p1. Turn.

Row 3 (RS): Slip 1, knit to 1 stitch before the gap created by the turn on the previous row, ssk to close gap (1 stitch from each side of the gap), k1. Turn.

Row 4 (WS): Slip 1, purl to 1 stitch before the gap created by the turn on the previous row, p2tog to close gap (1 stitch from each side of the gap), p1. Turn.

Repeat rows 3 and 4 until all stitches have been worked, ending with a wrong-side row—19 (21, 23) heel stitches remain.

Gussets

Return to working in the round, as follows: With the right side facing, knit across the 19 (21, 23) heel stitches, pick up and knit 15 (18, 21) stitches along the edge of the heel flap, place marker, work Chart D (page 113) *beginning with round 9 (5, 1)* over the instep stitches, place marker, pick up and knit 15 (18, 21) stitches along the other edge of the heel flap, knit the first 10 (11, 12) heel stitches, and place marker to indicate new end of round—76 (88, 100) stitches total.

Round 1: Knit to the marker, slip marker, work Chart D as established to the next marker, slip marker, knit to the end of the round.

Repeat the last round until you have completed round 24 of the chart. [Note that the gusset decreases occur within Chart D and Chart E (page 113), so the number of stitches on the instep will decrease as you work through these charts.]

Rearrange the markers as follows: Move the first instep marker 5 stitches to the right, and move the second instep marker 5 stitches to the left.

Next round: Knit to the marker, slip marker, work Chart E to the next marker, slip marker, knit to the end of the round.

Repeat the last round until all rounds of Chart E are complete. There are 60 (68, 76) total stitches.

Foot

Work in stockinette on all stitches until the foot measures 1½ (2, 2½)" 4 (5, 6.5 cm) less than the desired sock length.

Toe

Arrange stitches so that each of the 4 needles has an equal number of stitches, with the round beginning at the center bottom of the foot. Then work the toe decreases as follows:

Round 1: On needle 1, knit to the last 2 stitches, k2tog. On needle 2, ssk, knit to the end of the needle. On needle 3, knit to the last 2 stitches, k2tog. On needle 4, ssk, knit to the end of the needle.

Round 2: Knit all stitches.

Repeat the last 2 rounds until there are 10 stitches on each needle—40 stitches total.

Next round (decrease round): *Ssk, knit to last the 2 stitches on the needle, k2tog; repeat from * 3 more times.

Next round: Knit all stitches.

Repeat the last 2 rounds until there are 6 stitches on each needle—24 stitches total. Then repeat just the decrease round until there are 2 stitches on each needle—8 stitches total.

Break the yarn, leaving at least a 6" (15cm) tail. Thread the yarn tail through a tapestry needle and run the tail through all 8 stitches twice.

Weave in ends.

Repeat the pattern to make a matching pair.

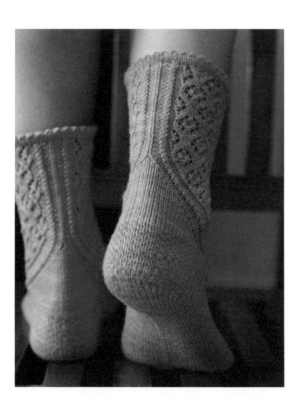
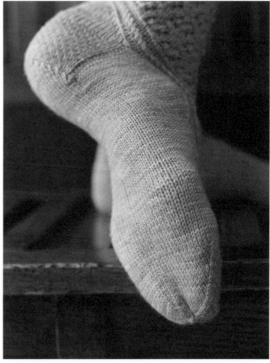

Isabella d'Este Charts

Key

☐ = K

⊡ = P

◩ = K2tog

◪ = P2tog

◪ = SSK

◪ = SSP

◪ = K3tog

◪ = P3tog

◮ = Slip next 2 sts together as if to knit them together, k1, pass the 2 slipped sts over the stitch just knit

◪ = Slip 1 as if to knit, k2tog, pass slipped st over

◯ = YO

■ = No Stitch

☑ = Insert tip of left needle from front to back into left leg of the st that is 2 sts below the st you just worked on right needle. Raise this stitch onto left needle and knit it.

◪ = Insert tip of right needle from front to back into right leg of the st below the next st on left needle. Raise this stitch onto left needle and knit it.

◪ = K2tog without removing sts from left needle, knit the first st again, remove both sts from left needle.

CHART A

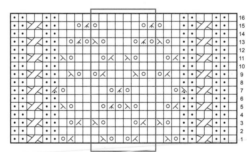

Work 5 (6, 7) Times

CHART B

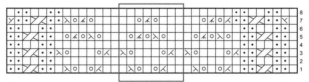

Work 4 (5, 6) Times

CHART C

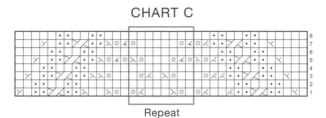

Repeat

CHART D

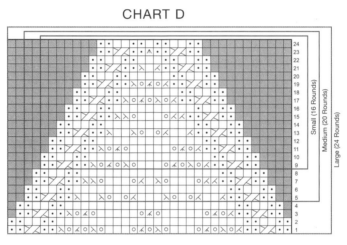

CHART E

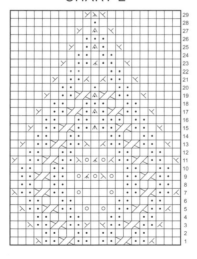

Tutu

Designed by Melissa Morgan-Oakes

Remember that ruling about yarn labels, the one that requires you to list anything less than 5 percent as "other fiber" unless it has a definite functional significance? Well, bling must provide functional significance because a host of sock yarns incorporate small amounts of sparkly silver in their content. (And no, not the color—the actual metal.)

The silver has been added not necessarily to warm or lend magical healing qualities. No, it's there to sparkle. And few things sparkle more than a pair of bright pink, girly-girl, ballerina socks. Version A (opposite) was knit in a plump, three-ply yarn that provides the perfect smooth surface off which the silver can pop. For those who want less bling and metal in their socks, Version B (pages 118 and 120) shows the same pattern in a ripply two-ply yarn that derives its shimmer and sparkle from the 30 percent addition of silk and a far smoother twist. Either way, these socks beg for pink.

SIZE
Women's M (L)

FINISHED MEASUREMENTS
Foot circumference: 7 (8¼)" (18 [21] cm) unstretched, to fit foot circumference of approximately 8¼ (9½)" (21 [24]cm)

YARN
294 (340) yd (269 [311]m) of fingering-weight yarn:
Sock A (left): 1 skein Black Bunny Fibers Stella Sock, 63% Merino, 20% silk, 15% nylon, 2% silver, 3½ oz (100g), 420 yd (384m), color Toe Shoes
Sock B (page 118): 2 skeins Shibui Knits Staccato Sock, 65% superwash Merino, 30% silk, 5% nylon, 1.8 oz (50g), 191 yd (175m), color 108 Cotton Candy

NEEDLES
1 U.S. size 1½ (2.5mm) 40" (101.5cm) circular needle, or size to obtain gauge

NOTIONS
Tapestry needle
3 stitch markers (including 1 locking stitch marker)

GAUGE
34 stitches and 46 rows = 4" (10cm) in stockinette stitch (knit in the round)

Notes

▸ *These socks are worked two at a time on one long circular needle, starting at the toes.*

▸ *This pattern uses the modified version of Judy's Magic Cast-On, which does not twist the stitches on the second needle (see page 187). If you are using the original version of this cast-on, you will need to adjust your stitches accordingly.*

▸ *All M1 increases should be worked using a backward-loop make 1 (see Stitch Guide).*

▸ *The Lace Rib Pattern and the Tiara Pattern can be worked using either the charts provided or the written directions in the Stitch Guide.*

▸ *See the Working Wrapped Stitches entry on page 190 for details about how to knit or purl a stitch together with its wrap.*

Stitch Guide

Cdd (central double decrease): Slip the next 2 stitches together as if to knit them together. Knit the next stitch. Pass the 2 slipped stitches over the stitch just knit.

M1 (backward-loop make 1): Using the working yarn, make a backward loop and place it on the right needle so that the working yarn points toward you.

Nupp: (K1, p1, k1, p1, k1) in same stitch. Then pass the first 4 stitches created over the last knit stitch.

Lace Rib Pattern

(Also see the Lace Rib Chart on page 121.)

Round 1: *K2, yo, ssk, k1; repeat from * to the end of the round.

Round 2: *K2, p1, k2; repeat from * to the end of the round.

Round 3: *K2, k2tog, yo, k1; repeat from * to the end of the round.

Round 4: *K3, p1, k1; repeat from * to the end of the round.

Tiara Pattern

(Also see the Tiara Chart on page 121.)

Round 1: Purl.

Round 2 (and even-numbered rounds 4–10): Knit.

Round 3: *K6 (9), (k2tog, yo, k1) 3 times, (yo, ssk, k1) 3 times, k5 (8); repeat from * to the end of the round.

Round 5: *K4 (7), (k2tog, yo, k1) 3 times, yo, cdd, yo, (k1, yo, ssk) 3 times, k4 (7); repeat from * to the end of the round.

Round 7: *K2 (5), (k2tog, yo) 2 times, k1, (k1, k2tog, yo, k1, yo, ssk, k2) 2 times, (yo, ssk) 2 times, k2 (5); repeat from * to the end of the round.

Round 9: *K6 (9), k2tog, yo, k1, (k2tog, yo, k1, yo, ssk, k1) 2 times, yo, ssk, k6 (9); repeat from * to the end of the round.

Round 11: *K11 (14), nupp, k1, yo, cdd, yo, k1, nupp, k11 (14); repeat from * to the end of the round.

Round 12: *K11 (14), ktbl, k5, ktbl, k11 (14); repeat from * to the end of the round.

Round 13: *K13 (16), nupp, k1, nupp, k13 (16); repeat from * to the end of the round.

Round 14: *K13 (16), ktbl, nupp, ktbl, k13 (16); repeat from * to the end of the round.

Round 15: *K14 (17), ktbl, k14 (17); repeat from * to

the end of the round.

Round 16: Knit.

Round 17: Purl.

Toes

Before casting on, arrange your yarn so that you have 2 ends to work with—1 for each sock. These yarn ends can be from 2 separate balls or from either end of the same ball if you're working from a center-pull skein. Using 1 end of the yarn, follow the instructions for Judy's Magic Cast-On (see page 187) to cast on 16 (18) stitches for the first sock onto 1 long circular needle. Slide these stitches farther onto the needles. Using the other end of the yarn, cast on another 16 (18) stitches onto the same needles for the second sock. Rotate your work clockwise so that both needle tips are pointing to the right and the smooth side of the work is facing you. The set of stitches on the right is the toe of sock A; the set of stitches on the left is the toe of sock B. Put a locking stitch marker into the right-most loop on the top needle (the first stitch of sock A). This marker will indicate when you have reached the end of a round, and it will help you distinguish sock A from sock B. Work in the round on both socks, as follows:

Round 1:

Side 1, socks A and B: Slide the stitches on the bottom needle onto the cable so that the bottom needle is free to be used as the working needle. Secure the yarn tail for sock A so that it passes between the working yarn for sock A and the top needle. Knit across the top 8 (9) stitches of sock A. Drop the yarn for sock A; pick up the yarn for sock B. Secure the yarn tail for sock B so that it passes between the working yarn for sock B and the top needle. Knit across the top 8 (9) stitches of sock B. Rotate your work clockwise again so that both needle tips are again pointing to the right and the smooth side is facing you.

Side 2, socks B and A: Slide the bottom stitches onto the bottom cable so that this needle now becomes your working needle. Then slide the top stitches onto the top needle so they are ready to be worked. Knit the next 8 (9) stitches of sock B. Drop the yarn for sock B; pick up the yarn for sock A. Knit the next 8 (9) stitches of sock A. You should be back at the marker, indicating that you have reached the end of the round. Rotate your work clockwise so that both needle tips are pointing to the right and arrange stitches on the needles so you are ready to work the next side.

Round 2 (increase):

Side 1, socks A and B: K1, M1, knit to 1 stitch before the end of sock A, M1, k1. Switch yarn. K1, M1, knit to 1 stitch before the end of sock B, M1, k1. Rotate work and arrange the stitches on the needles to prepare to work side 2 of both socks.

Side 2, socks B and A: K1, M1, knit to 1 stitch before the end of sock B, M1, k1. Switch yarn. K1, M1, knit to 1 stitch before the end of sock A, M1, k1. Rotate your work and arrange stitches to prepare for the next round.

Repeat round 2 for 5 (6) more times—40 (46) stitches total on each sock. Be sure to end each round back at the marker on sock A.

Next round: Knit both sides of both socks with no increases.

Next round (increase): Repeat round 2.

Repeat the last 2 rounds 4 (5) more times—60 (70) stitches total on each sock.

Feet

Next round:

> **Side 1 (instep), socks A and B:** Work in the Lace Rib Pattern across the 30 (35) stitches on side 1 of each sock.
>
> **Side 2 (sole), socks B and A:** Work all stitches in stockinette stitch (knit all stitches).

Repeat the last round, continuing to work side 1 (the instep) of both socks in the Lace Rib Pattern, while keeping side 2 (the sole) of both socks in stockinette stitch until the work measures 4 (4½)" (10 [11.5]cm) less than the desired sock length. End the work back at the marker on sock A.

Gussets

Round 1 (increase):

> **Side 1 (instep), socks A and B:** Continue to work in the Lace Rib Pattern as established.
>
> **Side 2 (sole), socks B and A:** K1, M1, knit to the last stitch of sock A, M1, k1. Repeat for sock B.

Round 2:

> **Side 1 (instep), socks A and B:** Continue to work in the Lace Rib Pattern as established.

> **Side 2 (sole), socks B and A:** Work in stockinette stitch on all stitches.

Repeat the last 2 rounds 14 (17) more times. Side 1 of each sock still has 30 (35) stitches, and side 2 of each sock now has 60 (71) stitches. Make a note of the last chart row worked on side 1.

Setup for Heels

Setup: This is a partial round, worked only on side 1 (the instep) of both socks.

> **Side 1 (instep) socks A and B:** Work in the Lace Rib Pattern as established. Rotate work and arrange stitches so that you are ready to begin working the heel on side 2 (the sole) of sock B.

Note: While shaping the heels, you temporarily switch to working the socks individually. You first work side 2 of sock B back and forth in short rows, then you work side 2 of sock A in a similar manner. When the heels are completed, you return to working both socks together in the round.

Heel of Sock B

Shape the heel cup of sock B, as follows:

Row 1 (RS): K15 (18), place marker 1, k29 (34), slip 1 purlwise, bring yarn to the right side to wrap the stitch, place marker 2 on left-hand needle, move the slipped stitch back to the left-hand needle. Turn work to the wrong side.

Row 2 (WS): Purl to 1 stitch before marker 1, slip 1 purlwise, bring yarn to the right side to wrap the stitch, move the stitch back to the left-hand needle. Turn the work to the right side.

Row 3 (RS): Knit to 2 stitches before the previously wrapped stitch, slip 1 purlwise, bring the yarn to the right side to wrap the stitch. Move the stitch back to the left-hand needle. Turn.

Row 4 (WS): Purl to 2 stitches before the previously wrapped stitch, slip 1 purlwise, bring the yarn to the right side to wrap the stitch, move the stitch back to the left-hand needle. Turn.

Repeat rows 3–4 until there are 4 (5) unwrapped stitches remaining at the center of the heel.

Next row (RS): K3 (4), slip 1 purlwise, bring yarn to the right side to wrap the stitch, move the stitch back to the left-hand needle. Turn.

Create the heel flap for sock B by continuing to work back and forth in rows on side 2 of sock B only, as follows:

Row 1 (WS): Purl, lifting the wraps and purling them together with their respective stitches as you come to them, to 1 stitch before marker 1. Then lift the wrap of the stitch before marker 1, slip purlwise both the stitch and the wrap to the right-hand needle, remove the marker, place the stitch and the wrap back on the left-hand needle, and purl together the wrap and its stitch along with the next stitch (as a p3tog). Turn.

Row 2 (RS): Slip 1 purlwise. Then knit, lifting the wraps and knitting them together with their respective stitches as you come to them, to 1 stitch before marker 2. Lift the wrap of the next stitch completely over and to the left of the stitch, slip the stitch as if to knit, slip the wrap as if to knit, remove marker, slip the next stitch as if to knit, place the 2 slipped stitches and the wrap back on the left-hand needle, and knit the 2 slipped stitches together with the wrap though the back loop. Turn.

Row 3 (WS): Slip 1 purlwise, purl to 1 stitch before the gap. (A gap will exist between the p3tog created in row 1 and the remaining gusset stitches.) P2tog to close the gap. Turn.

Row 4 (RS): *Slip 1 purlwise, k1; repeat from * to 1 stitch before the gap, ssk to close the gap. Turn.

Row 5 (WS): Slip 1 purlwise, purl to 1 stitch before the gap, p2tog to close the gap. Turn.

Repeat rows 4 and 5 until you have decreased away all the gusset stitches on side 2 of this sock. End having completed a right-side row. Side 2 of sock B now has 30 (35) stitches.

Heel of Sock A

To shape the heel cup and work the heel flap of sock A, repeat the instructions for sock B above. Each sock now has 60 (70) stitches total, with 30 (35) stitches on each side.

Legs

Return to working in the round on all stitches of both socks, as follows:

Next round:

   Side 1, socks A and B: Pick up a stitch where the heel stitches of sock A meet the instep stitches of sock A. Move the picked-up stitch back to the left-hand needle and knit it together with the first instep stitch. Work across the remaining instep stitches in the Lace Rib Pattern as established to 1 stitch before the end of side 1 of sock A. Slip the next stitch as to knit to the right-hand needle. Pick up another stitch where the instep stitches of sock A meet the heel stitches of sock A. Move the picked-up stitch and the slipped stitch back to the left-hand needle and knit them together through the back loop. Repeat for sock B.

Side 2, socks B and A: Work these stitches in Lace Rib Pattern, following the same chart row used for side 1.

Continue to work in the round, following the Lace Rib Pattern on all stitches, until the leg measurement from the top of the heel flap is 2½" (6.5cm).

Size Small Only

Next round:

    Side 1, socks A and B: Purl to 2 stitches before the end of sock A, p2tog. Repeat for sock B.

    Side 2, socks B and A: Purl to 2 stitches before the end of sock B, p2tog. Repeat for sock A—58 stitches on each sock.

Size Large only

Next round: Purl all stitches—70 stitches on each sock.

All Sizes

Work in the Tiara Pattern on all stitches for 17 rounds (1 repeat of the chart).

Next round:

    Side 1, socks A and B: Purl to the end of sock A, M1. Repeat for sock B.

    Side 2, socks B and A: Purl to the end sock B, M1. Repeat for sock A—60 (72) stitches on each sock.

Cuffs

Work 4 rounds of stockinette stitch.

Next round (picot turning round): *K2, yo, k2tog; repeat from * to the end of the round.

Work 4 rounds of stockinette stitch.

Loosely bind off all stitches of both socks. Turn the last 4 rounds to the wrong side along the picot turning round; stitch the bound-off edge loosely to the inside of the sock to create a hem.

Weave in ends.

Repeat the pattern to make a matching pair.

Tutu Charts

Key

☐ = K

⊡ = P

⊠ = Knit through the back loop

⊠ = K2tog

⊠ = SSK

⊙ = YO

⚄ = Slip next 2 sts together as if to knit them together, k1, pass the 2 slipped sts over the stitch just knit

N = (K1, p1, k1, p1, k1) in same stitch, pass the first 4 sts created over the last knit stitch

LACE RIB CHART

5-Stitch Repeat

TIARA CHART

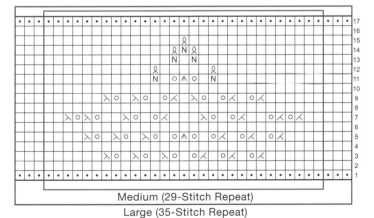

Medium (29-Stitch Repeat)

Large (35-Stitch Repeat)

Lady Tryamour

Designed by Sivia Harding

I first asked Sivia to design a durable lace sock, the kind of deeply pleasurable indulgence we could slip onto our feet in the morning and secretly smile about all day. The more she knit with this naturally dyed three-ply Merino yarn, the more the yarn's round, three-dimensional quality spoke to her. She was also wooed by its rich, creamy buttercup yellow.

The resulting sock is a perfect pairing of yarn and pattern with the yarn's fine gauge providing extraordinary stitch detail. Leafy tendrils march up the foot along slender vines of single twisted knit stitches that seem to hover over their reverse-stockinette-stitch background. Along the self-folding cuff, larger leaves make their way to the edge, where tiny leaves extend beyond the cuff and—in a touch that is pure Sivia—are adorned with tiny silver charms. Lest your heel should feel left out, Sivia also dotted it with one solitary leaf. The design has such a delicate, dreamy quality that I envision it fitting for Lady Tryamour, the beautiful fairy queen in the medieval tale of Sir Launfal.

In choosing yarns for this sock, be sure to use yarns with three or more plies, and try to stick with soft, hand-dyed colors that have faintly shifting degrees of saturation. A multicolor yarn would totally obscure the exquisite detail, while a solid would lack the flickering depth that makes these socks so magical.

SIZE
Women's S (M, L)

FINISHED MEASUREMENTS
Foot circumference: 6 (7, 8)" (15 [18, 20.5]cm) unstretched, to fit foot circumference of about 7½ (8½, 9½)" (19 [21.5, 24]cm)

YARN
360 (440, 530) yd (330 [402, 485]m) of fingering-weight yarn: 1 skein Swans Island Yarns Fingering, 100% certified organic Merino, 3½ oz (100g), 580 yd (530m), color Maize

NEEDLES
Set of 4 U.S. size 1 (2.25mm) double-pointed needles, or size to obtain gauge

NOTIONS
2 (4, 6) Hill Tribe silver leaf charms, available from Artbeads.com as item #HTS343
Stitch markers
Tapestry needle

GAUGE
37 stitches and 53 rows = 4" (10cm) in stockinette stitch (knit in the round)

Notes

▸ *If you find the standard M1 increases difficult to work on the toe, try using a backward-loop M1 instead (see page 116).*

▸ *See the Working Wrapped Stitches entry on page 190 for details about how to knit or purl a stitch together with its wrap.*

▸ *Slipped stitches are slipped as if to purl, with the yarn held to the wrong side of the work.*

Stitch Guide

M1: Pick up the bar between the stitches from front to back, and knit into the back of the picked-up stitch.

M1P: Pick up the bar between the stitches from front to back, and purl into the back of the picked-up stitch.

Sk2p: Slip 1 stitch as if to knit, k2tog, pass slipped stitch over.

W&T (wrap and turn): If you're working a knit row, bring yarn to the front of the work, transfer the next stitch from the left needle to the right needle, bring the yarn to the back of the work, replace the stitch on the left needle, turn. If you're working a purl row, bring the yarn to the back of the work, transfer the next stitch from the left needle to the right needle, bring the yarn to the front of the work, replace the stitch on the left needle, turn.

Toe

Using Judy's Magic Cast-On (see page 187) or your preferred toe-up cast-on method, cast on 22 stitches, or 11 stitches on each of 2 needles. The first 11 stitches are the instep stitches; the next 11 stitches are the sole stitches. Place markers, if desired, to indicate the end of the round and the boundary between the instep and the sole stitches.

Knit 1 round.

Work rounds 1 through 3 (7, 11) of Toe Chart A (page 130), then work all rounds of Toe Chart B (page 130).

When Toe Chart B is complete, there will be 29 (33, 37) stitches on the instep and 29 (33, 37) stitches on the sole—58 (66, 74) stitches total.

Foot

Work the Instep Chart (page 128) over the instep stitches and knit across the sole stitches, until the work

measures 3¼ (3⅜, 3½)" (8 [8.5, 9]cm) less than the desired sock length. On the last round, M1 somewhere on the sole—30 (34, 38) stitches on the sole, 59 (67, 75) stitches total.

Gusset Increases

Round 1: Continue to work the Instep Chart as established over the 29 (33, 37) instep stitches, k1, M1, knit to the last stitch, M1, k1.

Round 2: Work in established pattern over the 29 (33, 37) instep stitches, knit to the end of the round.

Work rounds 1 and 2 a total of 12 times, then work round 1 once more—56 (60, 64) sole stitches, 85 (93, 101) stitches total.

Turn Heel

Work in pattern over the 29 (33, 37) instep stitches, then hold these stitches aside to be worked later for the leg. Make a note of the last round worked of the Instep Chart.

Work back and forth in rows on sole stitches only, as follows:

Row 1 (RS): Knit 42 (45, 48), W&T.

Row 2 (WS): Purl 28 (30, 32), W&T.

Row 3 (RS): Knit 27 (29, 31), W&T.

Row 4 (WS): Purl 26 (28, 30), W&T.

Continue as established, working one less stitch on each row, until 12 stitches remain unwrapped at the center of the heel, with 9 (10, 11) wrapped stitches and 13 (14, 15) gusset stitches on each side; end having worked a wrong-side row.

Next row (RS): K12, pick up wraps on the next 8 (9, 10) stitches and knit them together with the stitches they wrapped. Pick up the next wrap and knit the stitch and its wrap together with the next unwrapped stitch (3 loops together), turn.

Next row (WS): Slip 1, p20 (21, 22), pick up wraps on the next 8 (9, 10) stitches and purl them together with the stitches they wrapped. Pick up the next wrap and purl the stitch and its wrap together with the next unwrapped stitch (3 loops together), turn—54 (58, 62) stitches on the sole; 30 (32, 34) stitches at the center of the heel; 12 (13, 14) gusset stitches on each side.

Back of Heel

Continue to work back and forth on the heel stitches, as follows:

Small Size Only

Setup row 1 (RS): Slip 1, p1, (ktbl, p2) 4 times, k2tog, (p2, ktbl) 4 times, p1, ssk, turn.

Setup row 2 (WS): Slip 1, k1, (ptbl, k2) 8 times, ptbl, k1, p2tog, turn—29 stitches at the center of the heel with 11 gusset stitches on each side.

Medium Size Only

Setup row 1 (RS): Slip 1, (ktbl, p2) 5 times, M1, (p2, ktbl) 5 times, ssk, turn.

Setup row 2 (WS): Slip 1, (ptbl, k2) 10 times, ptbl, p2tog, turn—33 stitches at the center of the heel with 12 gusset stitches on each side.

Large Size Only

Setup row 1 (RS): Slip 1, (p2, ktbl) twice, p2, M1, (p2, ktbl) twice, p2, M1, (p2, ktbl) twice, p2, M1, (p2, ktbl) twice, p2, ssk, turn.

Setup row 2 (WS): Slip 1, (k2, ptbl) 11 times, k2, p2tog, turn—37 stitches at the center of the heel with 13 gusset stitches at each side.

All Sizes

Row 1 (RS): Slip 1, follow odd-numbered rows 1–15 of the Heel Chart (page 129), ssk, turn.

Row 2 (WS): Slip 1, follow even-numbered rows 2–16 of the Heel Chart, p2tog, turn.

Repeat the last 2 rows until rows 1–16 of the Heel Chart have been completed. Then work row 15 of the Heel Chart on each right-side row and row 16 of the Heel Chart on each wrong-side row while continuing to work decreases as established, until 1 unworked gusset stitch remains on each side of the heel stitches. End having worked a wrong-side row.

Leg

Resume working in the round as follows: With right side facing, slip 1, work row 15 of the Heel Chart over the next 27 (31, 35) stitches, ssk. Work the next 29 (33, 37) instep stitches in established pattern (continuing with the next round of the Instep Chart), k2tog, work across the next 27 (31, 35) stitches following row 15 of the Heel Chart, k1—58 (66, 74) stitches total, with 29 (33, 37) stitches on both the instep and the heel.

Round 1: Continue to work the Instep Chart over the first 29 (33, 37) stitches, k1, work row 15 of the Heel Chart over the next 27 (31, 35) stitches, k1.

Repeat the last round until the current repeat of the Instep Chart is complete, then continue as established until 1 additional repeat of rounds 1–20 of the Instep Chart is complete.

Next round: Work round 20 of the Instep Chart over the first 29 (33, 37) stitches, k1, work row 15 of the Heel Chart over the next 27 (31, 35) stitches, k1.

Repeat the last round until the leg measures about 5" (12.5cm) from the top of the gusset.

Right Sock Only

Purl 27 stitches, place marker to indicate a new end of round. Work rounds 1–21 of the Right Cuff Chart (page 129).

Both Socks

After completing round 21 of the chart, bind off all but the leaf pattern stitches as follows: *Bind off stitches loosely in pattern following round 22 of the chart, up to the first stitch of the leaf pattern, knit the first leaf stitch and pass the previously worked purl stitch over it to bind the purl stitch off, then knit the 4 remaining leaf stitches; repeat from * until all leaf pattern stitches have been worked, bind off to the end of the round. Five stitches should remain for each hanging leaf—5 (10, 15) stitches. Cut the yarn and draw it through the final loop. Complete each of the 1 (2, 3) hanging leaves as follows: Attach yarn at the right-hand side of a 5-stitch leaf, ssk, k1, k2tog, turn; slip 1, p2, turn; sk2p. Cut the yarn, leaving an 8" (20.3cm) tail and draw it through the final loop. String the leaf charm onto the tail and weave in the end firmly. Repeat for each hanging leaf.

Weave in remaining ends. Turn the sock right-side out and fold down the cuff along the stockinette band. Repeat the pattern to make a matching pair.

Cuff

Turn the work inside out so that the wrong side of the work is on the outside, and change the direction of knitting. Rounds will now begin with the stitches at the back of the leg instead of the stitches at the front of the leg.

Round 1: Purl across the 29 (33, 37) back-of-leg stitches, M1P 1 (0,1) time, purl across the 29 (33, 37) front-of-leg stitches, M1P 1 (0, 0) time—60 (66, 75) stitches total.

Rounds 2–5: Purl.

Left Sock Only

Purl 3 (6, 9) stitches, place marker to indicate a new end of round. Work rounds 1–21 of the Left Cuff Chart (page 129).

Lady Tryamour Charts

Key

☐ = K on RS, P on WS

☑ = P on RS, K on WS

ℛ = Ktbl on RS, Ptbl on WS

⊠ = K2tog

⊠ = SSK

⊼ = Slip 1 as if to knit, k2tog, pass slipped st over

☑ = M1: Pick up bar between sts from front to back, k into back of picked-up st

⊞ = M1 for small size, K1 for other sizes

◯ = YO

■ = No Stitch

= K1, p1, k1, p1, k1 in 1 stitch

Note: Main charts include blocks of color that reference either the Bud Chart or Leaf Chart. When you reach such a color, simply refer to that color's smaller chart and work it into the pattern as indicated.

INSTEP CHART

BUD CHART

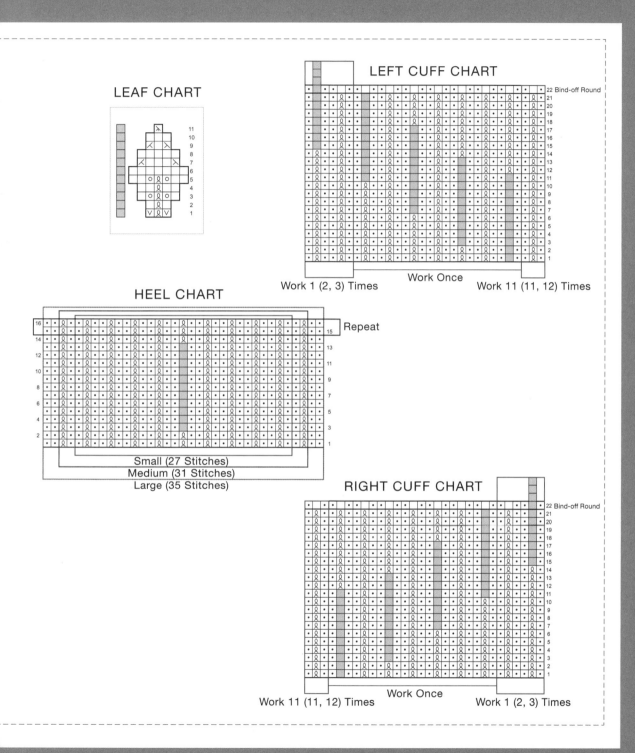

LEAF CHART

LEFT CUFF CHART

22 Bind-off Round

Work 1 (2, 3) Times   Work Once   Work 11 (11, 12) Times

HEEL CHART

Repeat

Small (27 Stitches)
Medium (31 Stitches)
Large (35 Stitches)

RIGHT CUFF CHART

22 Bind-off Round

Work 11 (11, 12) Times   Work Once   Work 1 (2, 3) Times

Lady Tryamour Charts

TOE CHART A

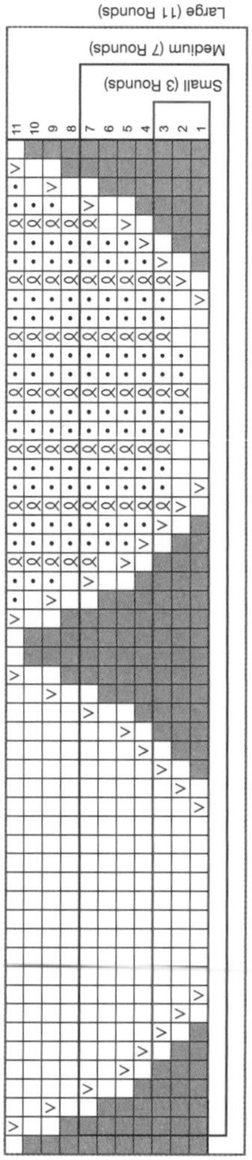

TOE CHART B

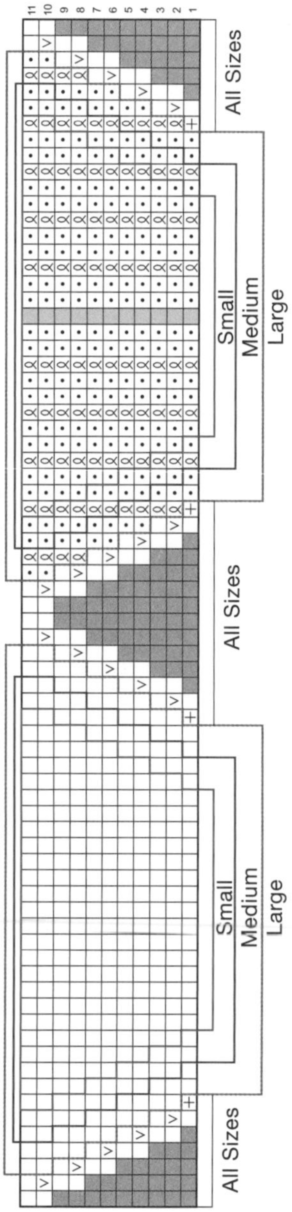

Kensington

Designed by Nancy Bush

Nancy Bush is a master at painting intricate scenes entirely from right- and left-crossing stitches—which is exactly what I asked her to do here. Everything you see—the elaborate fine lines of lattice-filled diamonds, zigzagging columns, and overlapping cables—are all optical illusions created much more easily than you'd think by using traveling stitches.

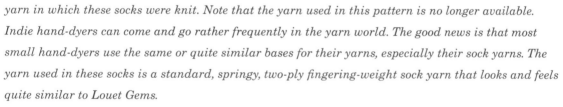

The liveliness and sense of rapid movement are enhanced by the tightly twisted two-ply Merino yarn in which these socks were knit. Note that the yarn used in this pattern is no longer available. Indie hand-dyers can come and go rather frequently in the yarn world. The good news is that most small hand-dyers use the same or quite similar bases for their yarns, especially their sock yarns. The yarn used in these socks is a standard, springy, two-ply fingering-weight sock yarn that looks and feels quite similar to Louet Gems.

All the traveling motifs are separated by single purl columns that give the cuff welcome elasticity while keeping the top of the foot reasonably smooth and comfortable. Still, because this pattern is filled with pairs of stitches that have been twisted over one another, you'll want to be sure to use a yarn with plenty of elasticity, whether from the twist, fiber content, or both. And by all means stick with solid and semisolid colorways, avoiding any jarring multicolored variegation that would overpower the intricate stitch pattern.

The socks get their name from the place in London where, over a fine meal at a French bistro, Nancy proudly handed me this finished pair.

SIZE
Women's M

FINISHED MEASUREMENTS
Foot circumference: 7" (18cm) unstretched, to fit
foot circumference of about 8¼" (21cm)

YARN
420 yd (384m) of fingering-weight yarn: 1 skein
Tactile: A Fiber Arts Studio Superwash Merino
Fingering Weight Sock Yarn, 100% superwash
Merino, 4 oz (115g), 437 yd (400m), color
Sagebrush

NEEDLES
Set of 4 U.S. size 0 (2.0mm) double-pointed
needles, or size to obtain gauge

NOTIONS
Tapestry needle

GAUGE
32 stitches and 48 rows = 4" (10cm) in stockinette
stitch (knit in the round)

Notes

▸ *Slipped stitches are slipped as if to purl, with the yarn held to the wrong side of the work.*

Stitch Guide

Skp: Slip 1 stitch as if to knit, knit the next stitch, then
pass the slipped stitch over the stitch you just knit.

Cuff

Cast on 68 stitches using Double-Start Cast-On method
(see page 187) or your preferred method for producing
a loose cast-on edge. Divide stitches onto 3 needles,
with 24 stitches on needle 1 and 22 stitches on needles
2 and 3. Join to work in the round, being careful not to
twist the stitches around the needles.
Work Chart A (page 136) on all stitches. Continue
working as established until all rounds of the chart
have been completed.

Leg

Rearrange the stitches so that there are 34 stitches on
needle 1, 15 stitches on needle 2, and 19 stitches on
needle 3.
Work Chart B (page 136) on the stitches on needle 1
(front of leg) and work Chart C (page 136) on the 34

stitches on needles 2 and 3 (back of leg). Continue in pattern as established, following both charts, until 4 repeats of Chart B have been completed, ending having completed round 18 of Chart B and round 6 of Chart C.

Heel Flap

Divide the first 34 stitches of the round onto 2 needles and hold them aside to be worked later for the instep. Place the remaining 34 stitches on 1 needle for the heel.

Turn work so the wrong side is facing. The heel flap is worked back and forth in rows, as follows:

Row 1 (WS): Slip 1, p33. Turn work.

Row 2 (RS): *Slip 1, k1; repeat from * to the end of the needle. Turn.

Repeat these 2 rows 15 more times, then work row 1 once more—33 total rows on the heel flap.

Turn Heel

Row 1 (RS): (Slip 1, k1) 10 times, skp. Turn.

Row 2 (WS): Slip 1, p6, k2tog. Turn.

Row 3 (RS): Slip 1, k6, skp. Turn.

Repeat rows 2 and 3 until all stitches have been worked, ending with a wrong-side row—8 heel stitches remain.

Gussets

Return to working in the round, as follows: With the right side facing, knit across the 8 heel stitches. Using the same needle, pick up and knit 16 stitches along the edge of the heel flap. With another empty needle, work row 1 of Chart B across the 34 instep stitches. With a third needle, pick up and knit 16 stitches along the other edge of the heel flap, then knit the first 4 heel stitches—74 total stitches (20 stitches on needle 1, 34 stitches on needle 2, and 20 stitches on needle 3).

Round 1: On needle 1, knit to the last 3 stitches, k2tog, k1. On needle 2, continue to work Chart B as established. On needle 3, k1, skp, knit to the end of the round.

Round 2: On needle 1, knit. On needle 2, work in pattern as established. On needle 3, knit.

Repeat these 2 rounds until 30 stitches remain on the sole (needles 1 and 3)—64 stitches total.

Foot

Continue to work in the round, keeping to the established pattern on needle 2 and working in stockinette stitch on needles 1 and 3 until a total of 6 repeats of Chart B have been completed (4 on the leg and 2 on the foot). (If your desired sock length is less than about 9¼" [23.5cm], work only 1 full repeat of Chart B on the foot.) Then continue as established for 17 more rounds, ending with round 17 of Chart B (do not work round 18).

Next round: On needle 1, knit. On needle 2, work Chart D (page 136). On needle 3, knit.

Repeat this round until Chart D has been completed. Then work in stockinette on all stitches until foot measures 1¾" (4.5cm) less than the desired sock length.

Toe

Move the first stitch on needle 2 to needle 1, and move the last stitch on needle 2 to needle 3—32 stitches on needle 2 and 32 total stitches on needles 1 and 3.

Round 1: On needle 1, knit to the last 3 stitches, k2tog, k1. On needle 2, k1, skp, knit to the last 3 stitches, k2tog, k1. On needle 3, k1, skp, knit to the end of the round.

Round 2: Knit all stitches.

Repeat these 2 rounds until 32 total stitches remain, ending with round 1. Then work round 1 only until 8 total stitches remain.

Move the first 2 stitches of needle 2 onto needle 1, then move the remaining 2 stitches on needle 2 onto needle 3. Graft the toe closed with Kitchener stitch. (Note that on this sock the grafting is worked from the bottom of the toe to the top, rather than from side to side.)

Weave in ends.

Repeat the pattern to make a matching pair.

Kensington Charts

Key

= K

= P

= K2tog

= YO

= Knit into back of second st without removing from left needle, knit into front of first st, remove both sts from left needle

= K2tog without removing sts from left needle, knit the first st again, remove both sts from left needle

CHART A

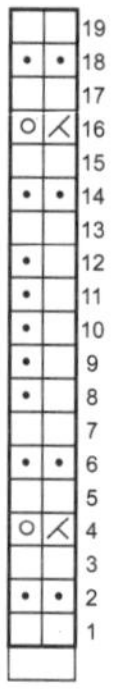

2-Stitch Repeat

CHART B

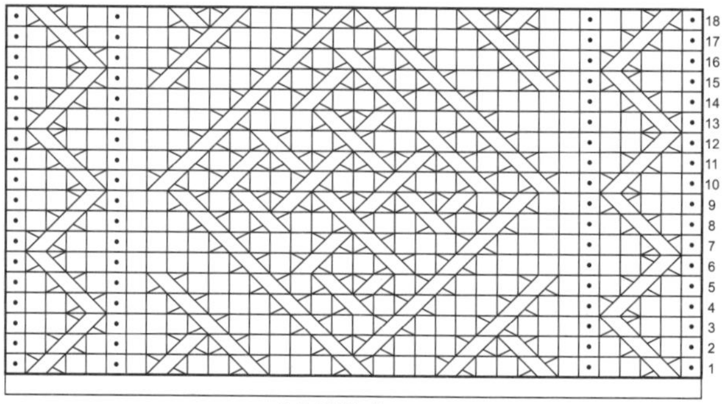

34 Stitches

CHART C

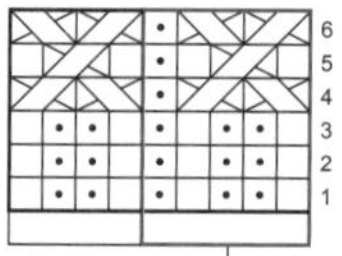

Work Once

Work 6 Times

CHART D

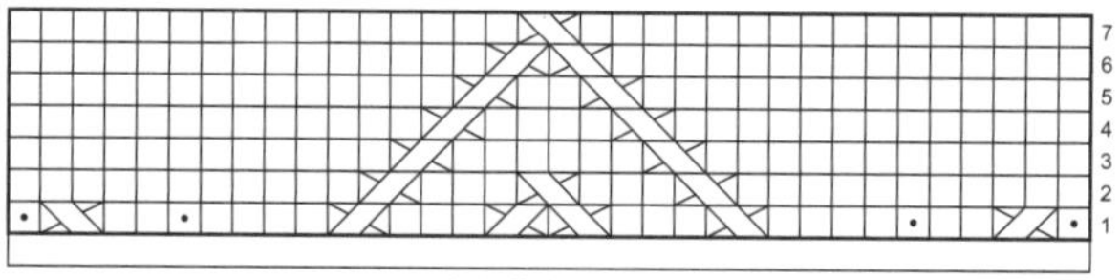

34 Stitches

Hummingbird

Designed by Sandi Rosner

Not every pattern can share the stage with a bright and variegated colorway. When colors change in knitted fabric, they usually produce horizontal lines that can stab otherwise lovely vertical sock motifs.

Here's a pattern designed expressly for all those gorgeous, hand-dyed, multicolored sock yarns in your stash, whether they are dyed in long stripes of color or in shorter bursts. The secret to this pattern is in breaking up the fabric surface so that each row—and the colors within it—can move up and down. Staggered decreases and yarn-overs swoop and dive between purl ridges, rather like the flight of a hummingbird when trying to impress its mate.

Sock A (above, right) uses a machine-dyed, self-patterning wool / nylon blend from Germany that's been infused with aloe vera and jojoba oils to keep your feet soft. The yarn's medium twist and gentle surface halo give the socks a somewhat soft, foggy sense of movement while the oils are said to remain in the fibers after more than 40 washes. Sock B (above, left) was knit out of a hand-dyed, variegated wool / nylon blend with a much tighter twist and firmer disposition, rendering the stitch pattern with much more crispness and clarity. Both socks welcome a touch of nylon to reinforce the short-row heels.

Be sure to experiment with yarns that have both long and short color repeats—each dye technique will render the stitch pattern in its own, slightly distinct way.

SIZE
Women's M

FINISHED MEASUREMENTS
Foot circumference: 7" (18cm) unstretched, to fit
foot circumference of about 8¼" (21cm)

YARN
350 yd (320m) of fingering-weight yarn:
Sock A (page 137, right): 1 skein Austermann Step
Easy, 75% superwash wool, 25% nylon, 3½ oz
(100g), 459 yd (420m), color 134
Sock B (page 137, left): 1 skein Mountain Colors
Yarns Crazyfoot, 90% superwash Merino wool,

10% nylon, 3½ oz (100g), 425 yd (389m), color
Moccasin Trail

NEEDLES
Set of 5 U.S. size 1½ (2.5mm) double-pointed
needles, or size to obtain gauge

NOTIONS
Stitch marker
Tapestry needle

GAUGE
36 stitches and 47 rows = 4" (10cm) in stockinette
stitch (knit in the round)

Notes

▸ *The Hummingbird Pattern can be worked using either the chart provided or the written directions
in the Stitch Guide.*

▸ *See the Working Wrapped Stitches entry on page 190 for details about how to knit or purl a stitch
together with its wrap.*

Stitch Guide

W&T (wrap and turn): With yarn to the wrong side of
work, slip the next stitch purlwise. Bring yarn to the right
side of work and move the slipped stitch back to the
left-hand needle. Turn work, ready to knit or purl in the
other direction.

M1R: Make a right-leaning increase by picking up the
bar between stitches from back to front and knitting into
the front of the picked-up stitch.

M1L: Make a left-leaning increase by picking up the bar
between stitches from front to back and knitting into the
back of the picked-up stitch.

Hummingbird Pattern
(Also see the Hummingbird Chart on page 143.)
Round 1: *P1, K2, P1, k2tog, k2, yo, k2tog, yo, (k1, p2,
k1) 3 times, yo, ssk, yo, k2, ssk, p1, k2, p1; repeat from *

to the end of the round.

**Round 2 (and all even-numbered rounds through
round 34):** Knit the knit stitches and yarn-overs, purl the
purl stitches.

Round 3: *P1, k2, k2tog, k2, yo, k2tog, yo, k2, (p2, k2)
3 times, yo, ssk, yo, k2, ssk, k2, p1; repeat from * to the
end of the round.

Round 5: *P1, k1, k2tog, k2, yo, k2tog, yo, k3, (p2, k2) 3
times, k1, yo, ssk, yo, k2, ssk, k1, p1; repeat from * to the
end of the round.

Round 7: *P1, k2tog, k2, yo, k1, yo, ssk, yo, k2, ssk, (p1,
k2, p1) 2 times, k2tog, k2, yo, k2tog, yo, k1, yo, k2, ssk,
p1; repeat from * to the end of the round.

Round 9: *P1, k2tog, k1, yo, k3, yo, ssk, yo, k2, ssk, k2,
p2, k2, k2tog, k2, yo, k2tog, yo, k3, yo, k1, ssk, p1; repeat
from * to the end of the round.

Round 11: *P1, k2tog, yo, k5, yo, ssk, yo, k2, ssk, k1, p2, k1, k2tog, k2, yo, k2tog, yo, k5, yo, ssk, p1; repeat from * to the end of the round.

Round 13: *P1, k2tog, k5, yo, k2tog, yo, k1, yo, k2, ssk, p2, k2tog, k2, yo, k1, yo, ssk, yo, k5, ssk, p1; repeat from * to the end of the round.

Round 15: *P1, k2tog, k4, yo, k2tog, yo, k3, yo, k1, ssk, p2, k2tog, k1, yo, k3, yo, ssk, yo, k4, ssk, p1; repeat from * to the end of the round.

Round 17: *P1, k2tog, k3, yo, k2tog, yo, k5, yo, ssk, p2, k2tog, yo, k5, yo, ssk, yo, k3, ssk, p1; repeat from * to the end of the round.

Round 19: *P1, k2tog, k2, yo, k1, yo, ssk, yo, k5, ssk, p2, k2tog, k5, yo, k2tog, yo, k1, yo, k2, ssk, p1; repeat from * to the end of the round.

Round 21: *P1, k2tog, k1, yo, k3, yo, ssk, yo, k4, ssk, p2, k2tog, k4, yo, k2tog, yo, k3, yo, k1, ssk, p1; repeat from * to the end of the round.

Round 23: *P1, k2tog, yo, k5, yo, ssk, yo, k3, ssk, p2, k2tog, k3, yo, k2tog, yo, k5, yo, ssk, p1; repeat from * to the end of the round.

Round 25: P1, k8, yo, ssk, yo, k2, ssk, p2, k2tog, k2, yo, k2tog, yo, k8, p1.

Round 27: P1, k9, yo, ssk, yo, k1, ssk, p2, k2tog, k1, yo, k2tog, yo, k9, p1.

Round 29: P1, k10, yo, ssk, yo, ssk, p2, k2tog, yo, k2tog, yo, k10, p1.

Round 31: K2tog, M1R, k10, yo, ssk, yo, ssk, k2tog, yo, k2tog, yo, k10, M1L, ssk.

Round 33: K13, yo, ssk, k2, k2tog, yo, k13.

Round 35: K14, yo, ssk, k2tog, yo, k14.

Round 36: Knit.

Cuff

Loosely cast on 64 stitches. Arrange 16 stitches on each of 4 double-pointed needles and join to work in the round, being careful not to twist the stitches around the needles.

Round 1: *P1, k2, p1; repeat from * to the end of the round.

Repeat this round until the cuff measures about 1¾" (4.5cm) from the cast-on edge.

Leg

Work rounds 1–12 of the Hummingbird Pattern, then work rounds 13–24 four times.

Next round: Work round 13 of the Hummingbird Pattern over needles 1 and 2 (the instep), work round 25 of the Hummingbird Pattern over needles 3 and 4 (the heel).

Continue as established through round 24 of the pattern on the instep and round 36 of the pattern on the heel.

Heel

Work round 13 of the Hummingbird Pattern over needles 1 and 2 and put these stitches on hold to be worked later for the instep.

Work back and forth in rows on heel stitches only, as follows:

Row 1 (RS): K30, W&T.

Row 2 (WS): P28, W&T.

Row 3 (RS): K27, W&T.

Row 4 (WS): P26, W&T.

Continue as established, working 1 less stitch on each row, until there are 10 wrapped stitches on either side of 10 unwrapped stitches at the center of the heel.

Row 21 (RS): K10, knit the next stitch together with its wrap, W&T (this stitch will now be double-wrapped).

Row 22 (WS): P11, purl the next stitch together with its wrap, W&T (this stitch will now be double-wrapped).

Row 23 (RS): K12, knit the next stitch together with both of its wraps, W&T (this stitch will now be double-wrapped).

Continue as established, working 1 stitch more on each

row and working the wraps together with their stitches, until all the single-wrapped stitches have been worked (1 double-wrapped stitch and 1 unwrapped stitch remain at each end of the heel needle).

Row 39 (RS): K28, knit the next stitch together with both its wraps, W&T.

Row 40 (WS): P29, purl the next stitch together with both its wraps, W&T.

Row 41 (RS): K30, knit the next stitch together with its wrap. Do not turn.

Foot

Resume working in the round, as follows:

Next round: Work round 14 of the Hummingbird Pattern across the instep stitches (needles 1 and 2), then work the sole stitches (needles 3 and 4) in stockinette stitch, knitting the first sole stitch together with its wrap.

Continue working in pattern on the instep (repeating rounds 13–24) and working in stockinette stitch on the sole, until 2 repeats of rounds 13–24 have been completed, ending with pattern round 24.

Work rounds 25–36 of the Hummingbird Pattern on the instep, keeping the sole in stockinette stitch.

When round 36 is complete, work in stockinette stitch until the foot measures about 1½" (4cm) less than the desired sock length from the back of the heel.

Toe

Round 1: *K1, ssk, k26, k2tog, k1, place marker; repeat from * once more.

Round 2: Knit.

Round 3: *K1, ssk, knit to 3 stitches before marker, k2tog, k1; repeat from * once more.

Repeat the last 2 rounds 6 times more—32 total stitches remain.

Work round 3 four times more—16 total stitches remain.

Move the instep stitches to one needle and the sole stitches to another needle, and graft the toe closed with Kitchener stitch.

Weave in ends.

Repeat the pattern to make a matching pair.

Hummingbird Chart

Key

☐ = K

⊡ = P

⊠ = K2tog

⊠ = SSK

⊠ = Pick up bar between sts from front to back, k into back of picked-up st

⊠ = Pick up bar between sts from back to front, k into front of picked-up st

⊙ = YO

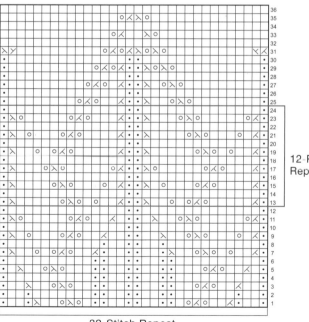

12-Round Repeat

32-Stitch Repeat

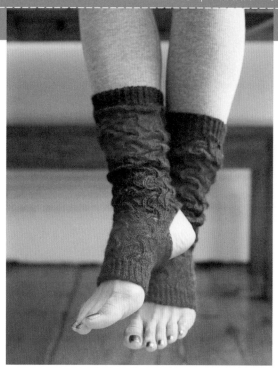

Prana

Designed by Cirilia Rose

Self-patterning sock yarns let us create elaborate color scenes without ever changing strands of yarn or even following a chart. But there comes a time when our hands get bored with the rounds and rounds of stockinette necessary to paint the picture the yarn manufacturers printed in the yarn. We long to throw in a few slip-stitch decreases here, some yarn-overs there, to liven things up. That's exactly what I asked Cirilia to do here with Sock A (opposite). The crafty pairing of increases and decreases creates a happy, churning swirl of stitches that complement color variegation without overpowering (or being overpowered by) it.

By virtue of having no heels or toes—the two areas that often get the most abrasion—these socks are also an ideal vehicle for any of the brightly colored singles sock yarns that otherwise might not last a month in your shoes. Sock B (above) shows these socks knit in one such yarn whose slow and gradual color changes thrive within the generous real estate of knitted fabric.

The pattern gets its name from the Sanskrit word for vital life force, or energy—used with the hopes that this energy will fortify the vulnerable singles yarn used in Sock B. The word is also commonly used in yoga, a context in which these socks in any yarn would be most welcome.

SIZE
Women's S (M, L)

Wolle Zauberball, 75% wool, 25% nylon, 3½ oz
(100g), 459 yd (420m), color 2082 [1 SUPER FINE]

FINISHED MEASUREMENTS
Calf circumference: 7 (8, 9)" (18 [20.5, 23]cm)
unstretched, to fit calf circumference of about 11½
(13, 14½)" (29 [33, 37]cm)
Foot circumference: 6¾ (7¼, 7¾)" (17 [18.5,
19.5]cm) unstretched, to fit foot circumference of
about 8 (8½, 9)" (20.5 [21.5, 23]cm)

NEEDLES
Set of 4 U.S. size 2 (2.75mm) double-pointed
needles, or size to obtain gauge
Set of 4 U.S. size 3 (3.25mm) double-pointed
needles, or needles 1 size larger than those used
to obtain gauge

YARN
**400 (450, 500) yd (366 [411, 457]m) of
fingering-weight yarn:**
Sock A (page 144): 1 (2, 2) skeins Berroco Sox,
75% superwash wool, 25% nylon, 3½ oz (100g),
440 yd (406m), color 1452 Bonham
Sock B (page 145): 1 (1–2, 2) skeins Schoppel

NOTIONS
2 stitch markers
Tapestry needle

GAUGE
30 stitches and 40 rows = 4" (10cm) in stockinette
stitch using smaller needles

Notes

▸ *The Scroll Lace Pattern can be worked using either the chart provided or the written directions in
the Stitch Guide.*

▸ *The larger needles are used to work the leg of the socks; the smaller needles are used to work the foot.*

Stitch Guide

Backward-loop cast-on: Using the working yarn, make
a backward loop and place it on the right-hand needle
so that the working yarn points toward you. Repeat until
you have cast on the desired number of stitches.

Scroll Lace Pattern
(Also see the Scroll Lace Chart on page 149.)
Round 1: *Ssk, k7, yo; repeat from * to the end of the
round.
Round 2: *Ssk, k6, yo, k1; repeat from * to the end of
the round.
Round 3: *Ssk, k5, yo, k2; repeat from * to the end of
the round.
Round 4: *Ssk, k4, yo, k3; repeat from * to the end of
the round.

Round 5: *Ssk, k3, yo, k4; repeat from * to the end of
the round.
Round 6: *Ssk, k2, yo, k5; repeat from * to the end of
the round.
Round 7: *Ssk, k1, yo, k6; repeat from * to the end of
the round.
Round 8: *Ssk, yo, k7; repeat from * to the end of the
round.
Round 9: *Yo, k7, k2tog; repeat from * to the end of the
round.
Round 10: *K1, yo, k6, k2tog; repeat from * to the end
of the round.
Round 11: *K2, yo, k5, k2tog; repeat from * to the end
of the round.
Round 12: *K3, yo, k4, k2tog; repeat from * to the end
of the round.

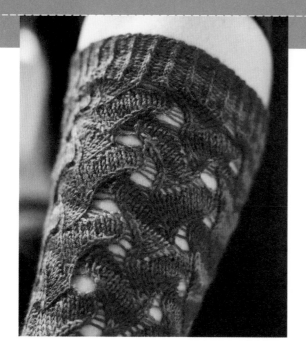
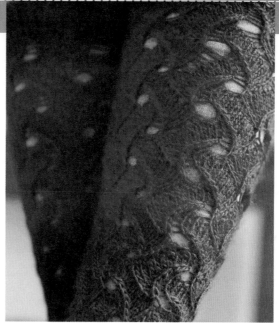

Round 13: *K4, yo, k3, k2tog; repeat from * to the end of the round.

Round 14: *K5, yo, k2, k2tog; repeat from * to the end of the round.

Round 15: *K6, yo, k1, k2tog; repeat from * to the end of the round.

Round 16: *K7, yo, k2tog; repeat from * to the end of the round.

Cuff

Using the larger-size needles, loosely cast on 64 (72, 82) stitches. Join to work in the round, being careful not to twist the stitches around the needles. Place marker to indicate the beginning of the round.

Round 1: *Ktbl, p1; repeat from * to the end of the round. Repeat the previous round until work measures about 1½" (4cm) from the cast-on edge.

Next round: *Ktbl, p1; repeat from * to 2 (0, 2) stitches before the end of the round, k2tog 1 (0, 1) time—63 (72, 81) total stitches.

Leg

Begin working the Scroll Lace Pattern on all stitches. Continue in pattern until the sock is the correct length to reach from your knee to the top of your ankle bone, or about 13" (33cm). End having worked any one of the following rounds of the stitch pattern: 2–4 or 10–12.

Heel Opening

Round 1: Work across 36 stitches in the Scroll Lace Pattern as established. Bind off the next 27 (36, 45) stitches very loosely to create an opening for the heel (bind off the final stitch over the first stitch of the next round).

Round 2: Work across 36 instep stitches in the Scroll Lace Pattern as established, place marker, then cast on 21 (25, 29) stitches for the sole using a backward-loop cast-on—57 (61, 65) stitches total. Join to work in the round, being careful not to twist the stitches around the needles.

Round 3: *Using the smaller needles*, work the instep stitches in pattern as established, slip marker, *ktbl, p1; repeat from * to 1 stitch before the end of the round, ktbl.

Repeat round 3 until the ribbing on the sole measures about ¾" (2cm).

Foot

Round 1: Work the instep stitches in pattern as established, slip marker, knit to the end of the round. Repeat the last round until the sole of the sock measures about 3" (7.5cm) or until the sole reaches about 1" (2.5cm) away from the base of your little toe.

Next round: *Ktbl, p1; repeat from * to 3 stitches before the end of the round, ktbl, p2tog—56 (60, 64) total stitches.

Next round: *Ktbl, p1; repeat from * to the end of the round.

Repeat the last round until the ribbing measures about 1" (2.5cm).

Bind off all stitches.

Weave in ends.

Repeat the pattern to make a matching pair.

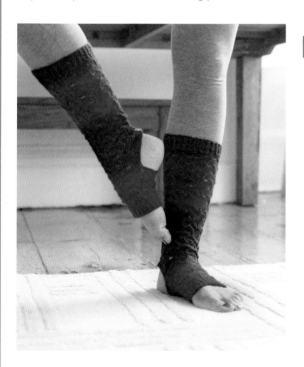

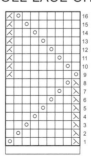

Prana Chart

Key

☐ = K

⊠ = K2tog

⊠ = SSK

⊡ = YO

SCROLL LACE CHART

9-Stitch Repeat

Strago

Designed by Jared Flood

Every other pattern so far has used a yarn spun in the worsted or semiworsted method for maximum durability. Does this mean you can't knit socks out of the fluffier, woolen-spun farm yarns? It depends on how you envision using the socks. Jared Flood proves the point with this thick and cozy pair of socks intended for padding around the house on cold winter days.

The use of two-color stranding on the leg and foot gives these socks an intentionally extra-warm, double-thick fabric. While the heels and toes are worked on smaller needles for greater durability, the sock may be too thick to fit in most shoes. But that's OK, because these are meant to be slippers, not everyday jam-in-your-shoe-and-go socks.

While stranded colorwork normally produces a notoriously inelastic fabric that can be tricky in socks, which rely on elasticity to give a good fit, Jared's woolen-spun yarn is extremely spongy and forgiving. As an added bonus, its fuzzy surface conceals any irregular puckering you may have in your colorwork—especially after you block the socks and let the fibers bloom in place.

SIZE
Women's L/Men's M

FINISHED MEASUREMENTS
Foot circumference: 9" (23cm) unstretched, to fit foot circumference of about 9½" (24cm)

YARN
300 yd (274m) of worsted-weight yarn: Brooklyn Tweed Shelter, 100% wool, 1¾ oz (50g), 140 yd (128m), 2 skeins of Long Johns (MC), and 1 skein of Fossil (CC)

NEEDLES
Set of 4 U.S. size 8 (5mm) double-pointed needles, or size to obtain gauge
Set of 4 U.S. size 6 (4mm) double-pointed needles, or 2 sizes smaller than needles used to obtain gauge

NOTIONS
Tapestry needle

GAUGE
24 stitches and 23 rows = 4" (10cm) in colorwork pattern on larger needles (knit in the round)

Notes

▸ *The solid-color sections of this sock (cuff, heel, and toe) are worked with the smaller needles. The colorwork sections of this sock (leg and foot) are worked with the larger needles.*

▸ *See the Working Wrapped Stitches entry on page 190 for details about how to knit or purl a stitch together with its wrap.*

Stitch Guide

W&T (wrap and turn): With yarn to the wrong side of the work, slip the next stitch purlwise. Bring yarn to the right side of the work and move the slipped stitch back to the left-hand needle. Turn the work, ready to knit or purl in the other direction.

Cuff

With smaller needles and main color (MC), loosely cast on 56 stitches. Arrange stitches on 3 needles and join to work in the round, being careful not to twist the stitches around the needles.

Round 1: *K2, p2; repeat from * to the end of the round. Repeat this round until the cuff measures 1" (2.5cm) from the cast-on edge.

Next round: Knit all stitches.

Leg

Switch to larger needles and begin working the Strago Chart on all stitches using main color (MC) and contrasting color (CC). Continue in pattern until you have completed 9 repeats of the chart, or as many complete repeats as needed to reach desired leg length. End having worked round 4 of the chart.

Heel

Work the first 29 stitches according to round 1 of the Strago Chart. Hold these stitches aside on needles 1 and 2 to be worked later as the instep. Drop CC (but do not cut yarn). Arrange the remaining 27 stitches on

needle 3 for the heel.

Using the smaller needles and MC only, work the heel back and forth in rows over the stitches on needle 3, as follows:

Row 1 (RS): Knit to 1 stitch before the end of the needle, W&T.

Row 2 (WS): Purl to 1 stitch before the end of the needle, W&T.

Row 3 (RS): Knit to the last unwrapped stitch (leaving it unworked), W&T.

Row 4 (WS): Purl to the last unwrapped stitch (leaving it unworked), W&T.

Repeat rows 3 and 4 until there are 11 stitches left unwrapped at the center of the heel, ending with a wrong-side row.

Row 5 (RS): Knit across the unwrapped stitches, then pick up the wrap of the next stitch and knit it together with its stitch, W&T (this stitch will now have 2 wraps around it).

Row 6 (WS): Purl across the unwrapped stitches, then lift the wrap of the next stitch and purl it together with its stitch, W&T so that this stitch has 2 wraps around it.

Row 7 (RS): Knit to the double-wrapped stitch, lift both wraps and knit them together with their stitch, W&T.

Row 8 (WS): Purl to the double-wrapped stitch, lift both wraps and purl them together with their stitch, W&T.

Repeat rows 7 and 8 until all single-wrapped stitches have been worked, ending with a wrong-side row. At this point, there is 1 double-wrapped stitch at each end of the heel needle.

Switch back to the larger needles and work row 1 of the Strago Chart over the next 26 stitches on the heel needle, *beginning with column 3 of the chart* and knitting the final stitch together with its wraps. Do not turn. The double-wrapped stitch at the other end of the needle will be worked on the next round.

Foot

Return to working in the round on needles 1 and 2 (the held instep stitches) and needle 3 (the heel stitches), using the larger needles for all stitches, as follows: Move the last stitch of needle 2 onto the beginning of needle 3—28 stitches total on needles 1 and 2, 28 stitches on needle 3. Work across the stitches on needles 1 and 2, following round 2 of the Strago Chart. Continue to work the chart across stitches on needle 3, picking up the wraps on the 2nd stitch and knitting them together with their stitch.

Continue to work the Strago Chart on all stitches until the foot measures about 1½" (4cm) less than the desired sock length; end having worked round 1 of the chart.

Toe

Switch to smaller needles, cut CC, and knit 4 rounds using only MC.

Round 1: On needle 1, k1, ssk, knit to the end of the needle. On needle 2, knit to the last 2 stitches, k2tog. On needle 3, k1, ssk, knit to the last 2 stitches, k2tog.

Round 2: Knit all stitches.

Repeat the last 2 rounds once more—48 stitches remain.

Repeat round 1 only 5 times—28 stitches remain.

Move stitches from needle 1 onto needle 2 and graft the toe closed with Kitchener stitch.

Weave in ends.

Repeat the pattern to make a matching pair.

Strago Chart

Key

■ = K1 with main color (MC)

□ = K1 with contrasting color (CC)

28-Stitch Repeat

Cape Spear

Designed by Lucy Neatby

A lot of people shy away from colorwork in socks because the conventional techniques produce form-fitting fabric that's low on elasticity. I knew that if anybody could create a colorwork sock that did have elasticity, it'd be Lucy Neatby. Sure enough, when I suggested the idea she immediately proposed this double-knit sock. The technique is a miracle worker, giving you the satisfaction of colorwork and durability, plus an extraordinarily plush and forgiving fabric. These socks are so thick that they tend to work best as house socks, though they may fit in certain kinds of shoes—especially clogs or mules with open heels.

The motifs were inspired by Native American trade blankets, and they are totally reversible. Worn with the "right" side out, the colorful pattern is set against a black background. With the other side facing out (opposite, far left and page 160), many more colors are anchored by a black stripe that runs along each side from toe to cuff. Or you can wear these as Lucy probably would, with one sock of each side facing out. A while back she and Cat Bordhi discovered they wore not only the same size shoe but the exact same kind, just in different colors. So they swapped one shoe each and still wear the mismatched pairs wherever they go.

Negative/positive two-color double knitting doesn't need patterning all the way around the sock in order to prevent long floats. In fact, there is no loss of elasticity anywhere, as there is not a single length of carried yarn anywhere in the sock. Although the leg and foot have the same number of stitches, the leg will fit a wider calf comfortably because the cast-on edge is double the normal number of stitches.

If you're not crazy about using multiple strands of different colors, consider working one main color and one strand of a nicely variegated yarn instead.

SIZE
Women's S (M, L)

FINISHED MEASUREMENTS
Foot circumference: 7¼ (7¾, 8¼)" (18.5 [19.5, 21]cm) unstretched, to fit foot circumference of about 8 (8½, 9)" (20.5 [21.5, 23]cm)

YARN
540 (625, 715) yd (494 [572, 654]m) of heavy fingering-weight yarn: Lucy Neatby Cat's Pajamas, 80% Merino, 10% cashmere, 10% nylon, 3½ oz (100g), 328 yd (300m), 1 (1, 1–2) skeins Black (M), 1 skein each Damson (A), Poppy (B), Dark Olive (C), Mango (D), and Turquoise (E)

NEEDLES
2 U.S. size 1½ (2.5mm) circular needles, or size to obtain gauge
2 double-pointed needles of same size or smaller

NOTIONS
Stitch marker
Tapestry needle
About 19" (48cm) of smooth scrap yarn in a contrasting color

GAUGE
28 stitches and 42 rows = 4" (10cm), counted on 1 face of the fabric in double knitting

Notes

▸ *These socks are worked in double knitting using 2 strands of yarn per round. The main color yarn (M) is used throughout the entire sock; the color of the other strand of yarn will vary as you work through the charts. For fewer ends to weave in, use a printed or handpainted yarn with a series of colors in sequence in place of colors A–E.*

▸ *With double knitting you construct an inner and outer face at the same time, both in stockinette. This makes the socks reversible. On these particular socks, the inner face will appear as a reverse image of the outer face.*

▸ *The stitches for these socks are worked mostly in knit/purl pairs. Within each pair of stitches the first stitch is typically knit in the color for the outer face of the sock, the yarns are moved, and then the next stitch is typically purled in the color for the inner face of the sock (which will appear as a knit stitch when viewed from the other side). The charts for this pattern show the stitches in these pairs; see the Stitch Guide for details about how to work them.*

▸ *Each square on the charts for this pattern represents a pair of stitches (1 for the outer face and 1 for the inner face). The background color of each square indicates the color for the first stitch of the pair; the color of the symbol inside the square indicates the color for the second stitch of the pair.*

▸ *Because these socks are reversible, all loose ends must be woven in so that they are not visible from either side of the work. When beginning or ending a new color of yarn, always leave a long tail. Secure these tails later by first linking them together and then duplicate-stitching them around a couple of matching stitches in opposite directions. Then slide the tapestry needle between the inner and outer layers of the sock for a stitch or 2 and duplicate-stitch another matching stitch. For additional security, thread the tail yet further between the layers before cutting off any remaining projecting tail yarn. This join is almost imperceptible.*

▸ Because these socks are reversible, they have 2 public or "right" sides (RS). However, for descriptive purposes the inner or far layer of the sock, as worked, will be considered the wrong side (WS).

▸ While working these socks, frequently check that no yarn floats are visible on the inside or outside of the sock (this would indicate that you have forgotten to move both yarns to the back or front of the work before knitting or purling a stitch). Both the inner and outer fabrics should look like regular stockinette stitch. Also, try to avoid twisting the yarns around one another accidentally (it helps to hold 1 strand in each hand).

▸ These socks are worked on 2 circular needles. When working in the round on 2 circular needles, use only 1 needle at a time. Let both ends of the resting needle hang down out of the way while you work with the other needle. Each needle is used to work only the stitches on that needle. Alternatively, these socks can be worked using double-pointed needles or 1 long circular needle.

▸ The 2 double-pointed needles are used only for picking up the double row of gusset stitches and for separating the inner and outer layers of the toe before joining.

Stitch Guide

Note: "X" designates color specified in chart.

kX/pX: With both yarns at the back of the work, k1 with the first color specified, move both yarns between the needles to the front of the work, p1 with the next color specified.

pB/kM: With yarn B at the front of the work and color M at the back, p1 with color B, k1 with color M. Do not move either strand of yarn between making these stitches.

s1wyib/s1wyif: With both yarns at the back of the work, slip the first stitch (a knit) purlwise, then move both yarns to the front of the work and slip the second stitch (a purl) purlwise.

sskX/p2togX: With both yarns at the back of the work, slip the first stitch (a knit) knitwise, let the second stitch (a purl) fall off the needle to the back, slip the third stitch (a knit) knitwise, replace the dropped purl stitch onto the left-hand needle. Replace both slipped knit stitches onto the left-hand needle and knit them through the back loops using the first color specified, as for a conventional ssk. Then move both yarns to the front of the work and purl the next 2 purl stitches together with the next color specified.

k2togX/sspX: With both yarns at the back of the work, slip the first stitch (a knit) purlwise, let the second stitch (a purl) fall off the needle to the back, slip the third stitch

(a knit) purlwise, replace the dropped purl stitch onto the left-hand needle. Replace both slipped knit stitches onto the left-hand needle and, using the first color specified, knit them together. Move both yarns to the front of the work, slip the next 2 purl stitches knitwise one at a time, and return them to the left-hand needle. Then, purl them together through the back loops using the next color specified.

Cuff

With color M, cast on 100 (108, 116) stitches onto 1 circular needle using the long-tail method (see page 188). Divide the stitches evenly between 2 circular needles and join to work in the round, being careful not to twist the stitches around the needles.

Setup round (optional): *K1, p1; repeat from * to the

end of the round. (This round is intended to help you establish the desired knit/purl stitch sequence before you begin the double-knitting technique. After this setup round, you will be knitting the knits and purling the purls on *most* rounds.)

Begin to work the Cuff Chart (page 162) on all stitches, as follows:

Rounds 1–3: KM/pA (see Stitch Guide), repeat to the end of the round. Cut yarn A.

Round 4: KB/pM, repeat to the end of the round.

Rounds 5–6: PB/kM, repeat to the end of the round. Cut yarn B.

Rounds 7–8: KM/pA, repeat to the end of the round. Cut yarn A.

Round 9 is written out in full. For this and all subsequent pattern rounds, follow the chart.

Round 9: *(KC/pM) 2 times, (kM/pC) 5 (6, 7) times, (kC/pM) 2 times, (kM/pC) 2 times, (kC/pM) 2 times, (kM/pC) 3 times, (kC/pM) 2 times, (kM/pC) 2 times, (kC/pM) 2 times, (kM/pC) 3 (4, 5) times; repeat from * once.

Continue working the Cuff Chart until all rounds of the chart have been completed.

Leg

Work all rounds of the Leg Chart (page 163).

Heel Flap

Partial round: (KA/pM) 2 times, (kM/pA) 24 (26, 28) times. Cut yarn A.

Rearrange stitches as follows: Place the next 54 (58, 62) stitches onto 1 circular needle and hold aside to be worked later for the instep. Place the remaining 46 (50, 54) stitches on the other circular needle for the heel. Turn work to the wrong side. The heel flap is worked back and forth in rows, as follows:

Row 1 (WS): S1wyib/s1wyif, (kC/pM, kM/pC) 10 (11,

12) times, (kC/pM) 2 times. Turn work.
Row 2 (RS): S1wyib/s1wyif, (kM/pC, s1wyib/s1wyif) 10 (11, 12) times, (kM/pC) 2 times. Turn.
Repeat the last 2 rows 14 (15, 16) more times. End having completed a wrong-side row.

Turn Heel

Row 1 (RS): S1wyib/s1wyif, (kM/pC) 13 (15, 15) times, sskM/p2togC, kM/pC. Turn.
Row 2 (WS): S1wyib/s1wyif, (kC/pM) 6 (8, 6) times, sskC/p2togM, kC/pM. Turn.
Row 3 (RS): S1wyib/s1wyif, (kM/pC) 7 (9, 7) times, sskM/p2togC, kM/pC. Turn.
Row 4 (WS): S1wyib/s1wyif, (kC/pM) 8 (10, 8) times, sskC/p2togM, kC/pM. Turn.
Row 5 (RS): S1wyib/s1wyif, (kM/pC) 9 (11, 9) times, sskM/p2togC, kM/pC. Turn.
Row 6 (WS): S1wyib/s1wyif, (kC/pM) 10 (12, 10) times, sskC/p2togM, kC/pM. Turn.

Row 7 (RS): S1wyib/s1wyif, (kM/pC) 11 (13, 11) times, sskM/p2togC, kM/pC. Turn.
Row 8 (WS): S1wyib/s1wyif, (kC/pM) 12 (14, 12) times, sskC/p2togM, kC/pM. Turn.

Size Large only

Row 9 (RS): S1wyib/s1wyif, (kM/pC) 13 times, sskM/p2togC, kM/pC. Turn.
Row 10 (WS): S1wyib/s1wyif, (kC/pM) 14 times, sskC/p2togM, kC/pM. Turn.

All sizes

30 (34, 34) heel stitches remain. Cut yarn C.

Gussets

With the right side facing, s1wyib/s1wyif, (kM/pD) 14 (16, 16) times across the remaining heel stitches.
The heel flap has a top and bottom layer. You can easily distinguish these layers at the edge of the heel flap, because the bottom layer stitches will be in color C, and the top layer stitches will be in color M. Pick up (but do not knit) stitches along the edge of the heel flap *separately for the inner and outer layers*, as follows: Take 1 double-pointed needle and slide it up into the outer leg of each of the slipped stitches on the bottom layer of the heel flap—15 (16, 17) stitches picked up. Then use another double-pointed needle to pick up an equal number of stitches on the top layer of the same edge of the heel flap.
Using the heel needle, work the picked-up stitches as follows: *Move both yarns to the back, ktbl the first picked-up stitch from the top layer using color M, move both yarns to the front, ptbl the first picked-up stitch from the bottom layer with color D. Repeat from * until all the picked-up stitches have been worked. Then, using the same needle, kM/pD the first pair of stitches from the instep needle.

Using the instep needle, (kD/pM) 2 times, (kM/pD) 8 (9, 10) times, (kD/pM) 5 times, (kM/pD) 8 (9, 10) times, kD/pM 2 times—2 stitches remain unworked on the instep needle. Work this remaining pair of stitches onto the heel needle as follows: kM/pD.

Using 2 double-pointed needles, pick up 15 (16, 17) stitches from each layer along the edge of the heel flap (as you did for the other side of the heel flap). Then, using the heel needle, work these stitches as you did previously.

Continuing with the heel needle, work across the heel and gusset stitches as follows: (kM/pD) 5 (6, 6) times, (kD/pM) 5 times, (kM/pD) 21 (23, 24) times. Place marker to indicate new end of round—144 (156, 164) total stitches, with 50 (54, 58) on needle 1 (the instep), and 94 (102, 106) on needle 2 (the sole).

Work the Gusset Chart (page 164) for the size you are making. When all rounds of the chart are complete, you will have 100 (108, 116) total stitches, with 50 (54, 58) stitches on each needle.

Foot

Work the Foot Chart (page 163) over all stitches. When all rounds of the chart have been completed, measure the length of the foot from the back of the heel. Add 1¾" (4.5cm) to this number (to account for the toe), and subtract this from the desired length of the finished sock to determine how many more inches you must work before starting the toe. Using this information, work whatever portion of the Foot Chart will fit. If you have room for 26 more rounds, work another full repeat; otherwise, work just a portion of the chart, such as rounds 4–20, rounds 7–17, or rounds 21–26. Alternatively, keep repeating rounds 24–26 of the chart using color M and whichever contrasting color you wish until the foot measures about 1¾" (4.5cm) less than the desired length of the sock. (The sample socks shown here have only 1 repeat of the Foot Chart worked on the foot.)

Toe

Work Toe Chart A (page 165) until all rounds are complete—60 (68, 76) stitches remain.
Work Toe Chart B (page 165) to completion—36 (44, 52) stitches remain.

Finishing

Cut yarns M and A, leaving a 24" (61cm) tail on each one. Then separate the inner and outer sock layers in preparation for grafting the toe, as follows: Thread a tapestry needle with a length of smooth scrap yarn in a contrasting color. Work across needle 1, sliding the knit

stitches onto 1 of the small double-pointed needles and the purl stitches onto the scrap yarn. Repeat for needle 2, using another double-pointed needle and the same piece of scrap yarn. The inner layer stitches (in color A) are now on the scrap yarn; the outer layer stitches (in color M) are now held on 2 double-pointed needles. Tuck the scrap yarn with the inner layer stitches and the inner layer yarn tail through to the inside of the sock. Using the color M yarn tail, graft the outer layer stitches together using Kitchener stitch.

Turn the sock inside out, slide the stitches from the scrap yarn onto the 2 double-pointed needles (dividing them equally between the needles), and graft those stitches together using the color A yarn tail.

Weave in loose ends so that they are not visible from either side of the work, as described in Notes.

Repeat the pattern to make a matching pair.

Cape Spear Charts

Key

Each square on the chart represents 2 stitches that are worked as a pair. See Stitch Guide for details on how to work these pairs of stitches.

▣ = kA/pM		▣ = kM/pA	
▣ = kB/pM		▣ = kM/pB	
▣ = kC/pM		▣ = kM/pC	
▣ = kD/pM		▣ = kM/pD	
▣ = kE/pM		▣ = kM/pE	
◩ = k2togM/sspA		◪ = sskM/p2togA	
◩ = k2togM/sspB		◪ = sskM/p2togB	
◩ = k2togM/sspC		◪ = sskM/p2togC	
◩ = k2togM/sspD		◪ = sskM/p2togD	
◩ = k2togM/sspE		◪ = sskM/p2togE	
▥ = pB/kM		☐ = No Stitch	

CUFF CHART

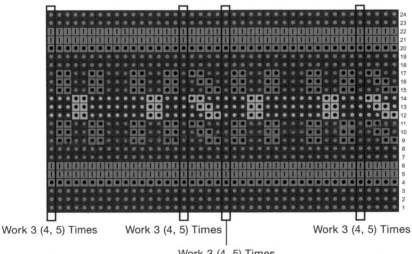

Work 3 (4, 5) Times   Work 3 (4, 5) Times   Work 3 (4, 5) Times

Work 3 (4, 5) Times

LEG CHART

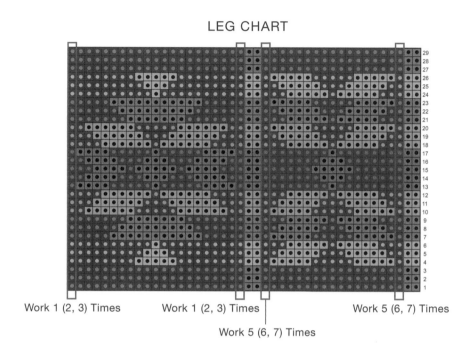

Work 1 (2, 3) Times   Work 1 (2, 3) Times   Work 5 (6, 7) Times

Work 5 (6, 7) Times

FOOT CHART

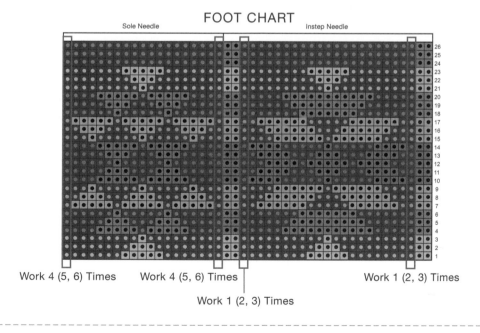

Work 4 (5, 6) Times   Work 4 (5, 6) Times   Work 1 (2, 3) Times

Work 1 (2, 3) Times

Cape Spear Charts

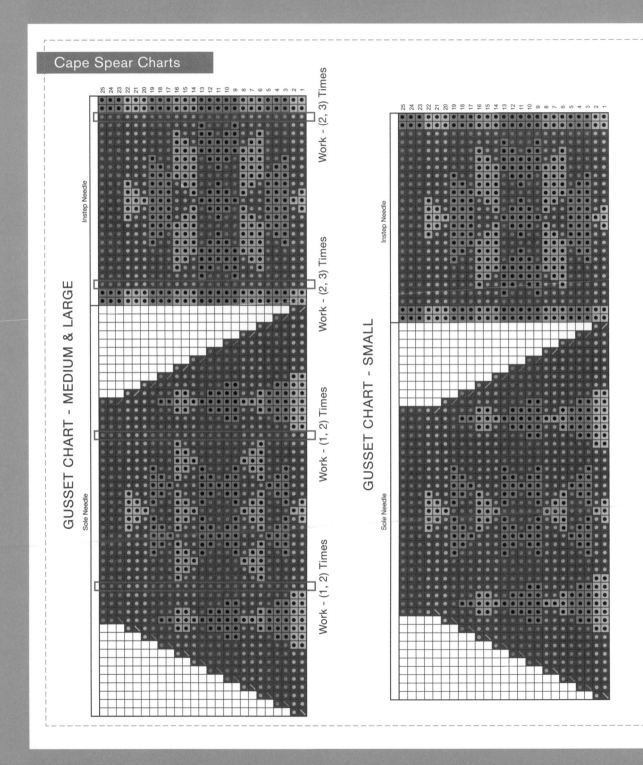

GUSSET CHART - MEDIUM & LARGE

GUSSET CHART - SMALL

TOE CHART A

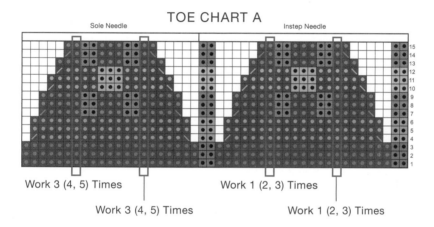

Work 3 (4, 5) Times

Work 3 (4, 5) Times

Work 1 (2, 3) Times

Work 1 (2, 3) Times

TOE CHART B

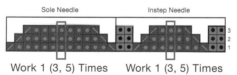

Work 1 (3, 5) Times   Work 1 (3, 5) Times

Percheron

Designed by Kathryn Alexander

Another way to render elastic colorwork is simply by changing the direction of your stitches. Kathryn Alexander is a genius at creating wildly energetic fabrics whose colors and stitches wiggle constantly as if they were living creatures, like the horses Kathryn raises in her upstate New York farm.

Kathryn makes this yarn for her designs using fibers from her brother's sheep and colors from her own dyepots. Colorwork plays such a central role in Kathryn's designs—her patterns often call for fourteen colors or more—that she sells her yarns in small bundles of skeins exactly for this purpose. While many of the socks in this book were intended to work with lots of different yarns, these socks were intended expressly for Kathryn's yarn. It's a soft but sturdy two-ply wool with sufficient twist to keep the longer wool fibers intact while still letting the fibers (and colors) bloom beautifully into one another with each washing and wearing.

The uniqueness of Kathryn's yarn makes substituting a challenge, but I do have an idea. What if you collected all your own leftover sport-weight sock yarn instead? You could use those different yarns to create this sock in your own personal crazy quilt of colors and textures, each of which will remind you of sock projects past.

SIZE
Women's M

FINISHED MEASUREMENTS
Foot circumference: 7" (18cm) unstretched, to fit foot circumference of about 8¼" (21cm)
Foot length: 9¼" (23.5cm) unstretched, to fit women's U.S. shoe sizes 7–9

YARN
325 yd (297m) of sport-weight yarn: Kathryn Alexander Designs, 100% Montana wool, 0.21oz (6g), 22 yd (20m), 5 skeins Dark Green (G), 4 skeins Brown (J), and 1 skein each Plum (A), Light Green (B), Burnt Orange (C), Turquoise (D), Gold (E), Rusty Orange (F), Rusty Rose (H), and Rose (I)

NEEDLES
2 sets of 5 U.S. size 2 (2.75mm) double-pointed needles, or size to obtain gauge
1 U.S. size 5 (3.75mm) double-pointed needle, or 3 sizes larger than needles used to obtain gauge

NOTIONS
Stitch holders or a small amount of scrap yarn to hold stitches not in use
Stitch markers
Tapestry needle

GAUGE
23 stitches and 41 rows = 4" (10cm) in stockinette stitch

Notes

▸ *The feet of these socks are very stretchy and should fit a wide range of foot sizes. However, if a longer sock is desired, extra garter-stitch rows can be worked at the beginning of the Toe section before starting the decrease round.*

▸ *Two sets of double-pointed needles are required to hold the stitches for the cuff and the leg when joining them together with a three-needle bind-off. The larger double-pointed needle is used only for working the three-needle bind-off.*

▸ *Slipped stitches are slipped as if to purl, with the yarn held to the wrong side of the work.*

Stitch Guide

Large Right-Leaning Triangle

Row 1 (RS): *With right side facing* and starting at the opposite end of the needle from where you ended with the previous color, attach color A and knit to the end of the needle. Turn.

Row 2 (WS): P2, turn.

Row 3 (RS): Slip 1, k1, turn.

Row 4 (WS): P3, turn.

Row 5 (RS): Slip 1, knit to the end of the needle, turn.

Row 6 (WS): Purl to 1 stitch past the gap created by the turn on the previous row, turn.

Repeat rows 5 and 6 until all stitches have been worked. End having completed a wrong-side row, but do not turn. Cut color A.

Large Left-Leaning Triangle

Row 1 (WS): *With wrong side facing* and starting at the opposite end of the needle from where you ended with the previous color, attach color B and purl to the end of the needle. Turn.

Row 2 (RS): K2, turn.

Row 3 (WS): Slip 1, p1, turn.

Row 4 (RS): K3, turn.

Row 5 (WS): Slip 1, purl to the end of the needle, turn.

Row 6 (RS): Knit to 1 stitch past the gap created by the turn on the previous row, turn.

Repeat rows 5 and 6 until all stitches have been worked. End having completed a right-side row, but do not turn. Cut color B.

Base Strip for Small Left-Leaning Triangles

Row 1 (RS): Attach color F and knit to the end of the row, removing all markers. Turn.

Row 2 (WS): Knit to the end of the row. Cut yarn. Do not turn.

Row 3 (WS): *With wrong side facing* and starting at the opposite end of the needle from where you ended with the previous color, attach color G and purl to the end of the row. Turn.

Small Left-Leaning Triangle

Row 1 (RS): Place marker, k2, turn.

Row 2 (WS): Slip 1, purl back to marker, turn.

Row 3 (RS): Knit to 1 stitch past the gap created by the turn on the previous row, turn.

Repeat rows 2 and 3 until 6 stitches have been knit past the marker on a right-side row. Do not turn. Do not cut yarn.

Base Strip for Small Right-Leaning Triangles

Row 1 (RS): *With right side facing* and starting at the opposite end of the needle from where you ended with the previous color, attach color H and knit to the end of the row, removing all markers. Turn.

Row 2 (WS): Knit to the end of the row. Cut yarn. Turn.

Row 3 (RS): Attach color G and knit to the end of the row. Turn.

Small Right-Leaning Triangle

Row 1 (WS): Place marker, p2, turn.

Row 2 (RS): Slip 1, knit back to marker, turn.

Row 3 (WS): Purl to 1 stitch past the gap created by the turn on the previous row, turn.

Repeat rows 2 and 3 until 6 stitches have been purled past the marker on a wrong-side row. Do not turn. Do not cut yarn.

Cuff

With the smaller needles and color A, cast on 9 stitches using a provisional cast-on method (this counts as the first right-side row). Turn work.

Follow the directions in the Stitch Guide to make a Large Right-Leaning Triangle, *starting with row 2*.

Change to color B, and make a Large Left-Leaning Triangle.

Change to color A, and make a Large Right-Leaning Triangle.

Continue to alternate working these 2 shapes in these 2 colors until you have completed 12 triangles. Do not cut yarn.

Connect the first and last triangles to form a circular band for the top of cuff, as follows: Remove the provisional cast-on from the first triangle and slide the 9 released stitches onto an empty needle. Fold the strip of triangles in half so the right sides are together and the cast-on edge is parallel to the last row worked. *Using the larger needle*, work a 3-needle bind-off (see page 190). Cut yarn. Turn the cuff right-side out.

Using the smaller needles and color C, pick up and

knit 7 stitches from the long edge of one of the color B triangles in the cuff. Then pick up and knit 2 stitches from the point of the adjoining triangle. Continue picking up stitches in this manner around 1 edge of the cuff— 54 total stitches picked up.

Work the lower part of the cuff in the round, as follows:

Round 1: Purl to the end of the round. Cut yarn.

Round 2: Using color D, knit to the end of the round.

Round 3: Purl to the end of the round. Cut yarn.

Repeat rounds 2 and 3 using color E.

Set the cuff aside while the leg is worked separately.

Leg and Instep

Using smaller needles and color F, cast on 48 stitches using a provisional cast-on method (this counts as the first right-side row). Turn work.

Follow directions in the Stitch Guide to create a Base Strip for Small Left-Leaning Triangles, *starting with row 2*. Then make a total of 8 consecutive Small Left-Leaning Triangles. Cut yarn.

Follow directions in the Stitch Guide to create a Base Strip for Small Right-Leaning Triangles, followed by a total of 8 consecutive Small Right-Leaning Triangles. Cut yarn.

Create a Base Strip for Small Left-Leaning Triangles, followed by a total of 8 consecutive Small Left-Leaning Triangles. Cut yarn.

Continue to alternate creating strips of Small Right- and Left-Leaning Triangles until you have created a total of 5 strips of triangles, ending with a set of Left-Leaning Triangles.

Create a Base Strip for Small Right-Leaning Triangles, *but do not work row 3*. With right side facing, move the first 30 stitches to a stitch holder or a piece of scrap yarn and hold them aside (these stitches will later become the instep). Then, using color G, knit the remaining 18 stitches. Turn and create a set of 3 consecutive Right-Leaning Triangles.

Continue to alternate creating strips of Left- and Right-Leaning Triangles to create 6 more strips of triangles, *but work only 3 consecutive triangles for each strip*. When complete, you should have a total of 12 strips of triangles (5 long strips and 7 short strips), and you should have ended with a set of Right-Leaning Triangles. Do not cut yarn.

Connect the first and last strips of triangles to form the leg of the sock, as follows: Remove the provisional cast-on from the first strip of triangles and slide the 48 released stitches onto an empty needle. With the right-side facing, place the leftmost 30 released stitches on a stitch holder or piece of scrap yarn and hold aside. Fold the work so the right sides are together and the cast-on edge is parallel to the final strip of 3 triangles. *Using*

the larger needle, work a 3-needle bind-off on the 18 stitches that make up these 3 triangles. Cut yarn. Turn the leg right-side out.

Connect the leg to the cuff, as follows: Hold the leg so the held instep stitches are pointing down. Using color I and the smaller needles, pick up and knit 54 stitches around the top of the leg (picking up 5 stitches from each long triangle edge, 2 stitches from each short triangle edge, and 1 stitch from each garter-stitch band). Purl 1 round. Turn the leg wrong-side out. Position the cuff inside the leg so that the right sides are together and the needles with live stitches are next to each other. *Using the larger needle*, work a 3-needle bind-off to connect the leg to the cuff. Cut yarn. Turn the piece right-side out.

Sole

Move the 30 held stitches on the left side of the instep (in color H) from the stitch holder back onto the smaller needles.

Row 1 (RS): Attach color D and knit to the end of the row. Turn.

Row 2 (WS): Knit to the end of the row. Turn. Cut yarn. Using color E, repeat the last 2 rows once more.

Attach color J and work in stockinette stitch for the sole, as follows:

Row 1 (RS): Knit.

Row 2 (WS): Purl.

Repeat the last 2 rows until a total of 32 rows of color J have been completed, ending with a wrong-side row. Cut yarn.

Next row (RS): Attach color E and knit to the end of the row. Turn.

Next row (WS): Knit to the end of the row. Turn. Cut yarn. Using color D, repeat the last 2 rows once more. Do not cut yarn.

Connect the sole to the instep to form the foot of the sock, as follows: Place the 30 stitches previously released from the provisional cast-on back onto a small needle. Fold the instep and sole in half so the wrong sides are together and the cast-on edge is parallel to the last sole row worked. *Using the larger needle*, work a 3-needle bind-off. Cut yarn. Turn the foot right-side out.

Heel

Using color F and the smaller needles, pick up and knit 64 stitches around the heel opening, as follows: Start at the middle garter-stitch ridge at the right side of the foot where the instep meets the sole, and pick up and knit 1 stitch from each of the 2 garter-stitch ridges at the side of the sole, 28 stitches along the edge of the stockinette-stitch sole, and 1 stitch from each of the next 2 garter-stitch ridges. Then, along the back of the

leg, pick up 1 stitch from each garter-stitch ridge, 2 stitches from the short edge of each triangle, 5 stitches from the long edge of each triangle, and 1 extra stitch from the garter-stitch ridge at the end of the round. Distribute the stitches evenly on 4 double-pointed needles, with the sole stitches on needles 1 and 2, and the back-of-the-leg stitches on needles 3 and 4.

Next round: Purl to the end of the round. Cut yarn. Change to color H.

Next round (decrease): On needle 1, ssk, knit to the end of the needle. On needle 2, knit to the last 3 stitches on the needle, k2tog, k1. On needle 3, ssk, knit to the end of the needle. On needle 4, knit to the last 3 stitches on the needle, k2tog, k1.

Next round: Purl.

Cut yarn. With color D, knit 1 round, purl 1 round.

Cut yarn. With color E, work 1 decrease round, purl 1 round.

Cut yarn. With color I, knit 1 round, purl 1 round.

Cut yarn. With color F, work 1 decrease round, purl 1 round.

Cut yarn. With color D, knit 1 round, purl 1 round.

Cut yarn. Then work 1 decrease round and 1 purl round with each of the following colors in turn: E, I, F, D, and E—32 total stitches remain.

With color I, knit 1 round, purl 1 round.

Move needle 1 stitches onto needle 2, and needle 3 stitches onto needle 4. Then graft the heel closed with Kitchener stitch.

Toe

Using color C and smaller needles, pick up and knit 60 stitches around the toe opening, as follows: Start at the lowermost garter-stitch ridge at the left side of the foot where the instep meets the sole and pick up and knit 1 stitch from the garter-stitch ridge, 28 stitches along the edge of stockinette-stitch sole, and 1 stitch from the next garter-stitch ridge. Then, along the instep, pick up and knit 1 stitch from each garter-stitch ridge, 6 stitches from each long triangle edge, and 2 stitches from each short triangle edge. Distribute the stitches evenly over 4 double-pointed needles, with the sole stitches on needles 1 and 2 and the instep stitches on needles 3 and 4.

Round 1: Purl.

Round 2 (decrease): On needle 1, ssk, knit to the end of the needle. On needle 2, knit to last 3 stitches, k2tog, k1. On needle 3, ssk, knit to the end of the needle. On needle 4, knit to the last 3 stitches, k2tog, k1.

Round 3: Purl.

Cut yarn. Attach color E and repeat rounds 2 and 3 two more times.

Then work rounds 2 and 3 two times for each of the following colors: color B, color J, and color A—24 total stitches remain.

Move all instep stitches onto one needle and all sole stitches onto another needle and graft the toe closed with Kitchener stitch.

Weave in ends.

Repeat the pattern to make a matching pair.

Turbo Toes

Designed by A. Karen Alfke

When I asked Karen how she'd create a truly indestructible sock, she thought for a minute, eyes darting to and fro as her mind worked, and then answered, "Linen-stitch toe?" Thus began this ingenious and unbelievably well-wearing sock that uses a combination of slip-stitch patterns you may not have considered for socks before.

Because slipped stitches tend to create a very dense, inelastic fabric, both samples are knit in the extraordinarily springy, nearly perpendicularly plied Socks That Rock Lightweight Yarn from Blue Moon Fiber Arts. Still, these socks are slightly denser than those made from simple stockinette or pure ribbing. But it's the price you pay for turbocharged, industrial-strength, handknitted socks.

Once you get one pair of these socks under your belt, you can lift discrete elements from this sock and use them to toughen up any other socks in your sock-knitting repertoire.

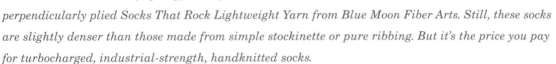

SIZE
Women's M (Women's L/Men's M)

FINISHED MEASUREMENTS
Foot circumference: 7¾ (8¼)" (19.5 [21]cm) unstretched, to fit foot circumference of about 8½ (9)" (21.5 [23]cm)
Leg circumference: 8 (8½)" (20.5 [21.5]cm) unstretched, to fit lower leg circumference of about 9½ (10)" (24 [25.5]cm)

YARN
360 (400) yd (329 [365]m) of fingering-weight yarn: 1–2 (2) skeins Blue Moon Fiber Arts Socks That Rock Lightweight Yarn, 100% superwash Merino wool, 4½ oz (127g), 360 yd (329m)
Sock A (above), in women's M: color Tanzanite

Sock B (page175), in men's M: color Obsidian

NEEDLES
2 size U.S. 1½ (2.5mm) 16" (40cm) circular needles, or size to obtain gauge
2 size U.S. 3 (3.25mm) 16" (40cm) circular needles, or 0.75mm larger than needles used to obtain gauge

NOTIONS
2 stitch markers
Tapestry needle

GAUGE
32 stitches and 45 rows = 4" (10cm) in stockinette stitch on smaller needles (knit in the round)

Notes

▸ *This pattern uses the modified version of Judy's Magic Cast-On, which does not twist the stitches on the second needle (see page 187). If you are using the original version of this cast-on, you will need to adjust your stitches accordingly.*

▸ *While working the slip-stitch patterns in these socks, be sure to move the working yarn into position (to the front or the back of the work as specified)* between *stitches to prevent accidental yarn-overs. Also, always slip stitches purlwise. This prevents the introduction of a twist into the stitch.*

▸ *These socks are worked on two circular needles. When working in the round on two circular needles, use only one needle at a time. Let both ends of the resting needle hang down out of the way while you work with the other needle. Each needle is used to work only the stitches on that needle.*

Stitch Guide

Kfb: Knit through the front loop of the next stitch but do not take it off the left-hand needle; knit through the back loop of the same stitch, then slip both stitches off the left-hand needle.

Slip 1 wyib: Move the yarn between the needles to the back of the work, and slip the next stitch purlwise. Then move the yarn into the correct position (front or back) for the next stitch.

Slip 1 wyif: Move the yarn between the needles to the front of the work, and slip the next stitch purlwise. Then move the yarn into the correct position (front or back) for the next stitch.

Toe

Using Judy's Magic Cast-On (see page 187) and the 2 larger circular needles, cast on 8 (10) stitches on each needle—16 (20) stitches total.

Setup round: On needle 1, *k1, slip 1 wyif; repeat from * to the end of the needle. Repeat for the second needle.

Round 1: On needle 1, kfb, *k1, slip 1 wyif; repeat from * to last stitch on the needle, kfb. Repeat for the second needle.

Repeat last round 3 more times—32 (36) stitches total.

Round 5: *Slip 1 wyif, k1; repeat from * to the end of the needle. Repeat for the second needle.

Round 6: Kfb, *slip 1 wyif, k1; repeat from * to the last stitch on the needle, kfb. Repeat for the second needle.

Round 7: *K1, slip 1 wyif; repeat from * to the end of the needle. Repeat for the second needle.

Round 8: Kfb, *k1, slip 1 wyif; repeat from * to the last stitch on the needle, kfb. Repeat for the second needle. Repeat the last 4 rounds 3 more times—64 (68) stitches total.

Round 21: *Slip 1 wyif, k1; repeat from * to the end of the needle. Repeat for the second needle.

Round 22: *K1, slip 1 wyif; repeat from * to the end of the needle. Repeat for the second needle. Repeat the last 2 rounds until the work measures about 2 (2½)" (5 [6.5]cm) from the tip of the toe.

Foot

Switch to the smaller needles and begin working in stockinette on needle 1 (the instep) and in pattern on needle 2 (the sole), as follows:

Round 1: Knit.

Round 2: Knit all stitches on needle 1. On needle 2, *slip 1wyib, k1; repeat from * to the end of the needle.

Round 3: Knit.

Round 4: Knit all stitches on needle 1. On needle 2, *k1, slip 1 wyib; repeat from * to the end of the needle. Repeat the last 4 rounds until the sole of the sock measures about 3½ (4)" (9 [10]cm) less than the desired length of the sock (when slightly stretched). End having worked a round 1 or 3.

Sole Flap

Knit across stitches on needle 1 (instep), then hold aside to be worked later.

Using the larger needles, work back and forth in rows on needle 2 (the sole), only to create a "heel flap" on the sole of the sock, as follows:

Row 1 (RS): *K1, slip 1 wyif; repeat from * to the end of the needle. Turn work.

Row 2 (WS): Ktbl, *slip 1 wyib, p1; repeat from * to the

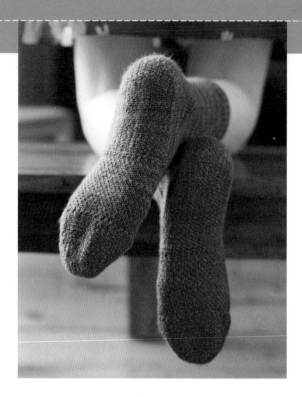

last stitch on the needle, slip 1 wyif. Turn.

Row 3 (RS): Ktbl, *slip 1 wyif, k1; repeat from * to the last stitch on the needle, slip 1 wyif. Turn. Repeat rows 2 and 3 until you have 18 slipped stitches along each edge of the heel flap—36 rows total in the heel flap. End having worked a row 2.

Turn Heel

Continuing to work only on needle 2 with the larger needle, turn the heel with short rows as follows:

Row 1 (RS): Ktbl, slip 1 wyif, *k1, slip 1 wyif; repeat until 10 (12) stitches remain on the left needle, bring yarn to the back of the work between the needle tips and turn (working yarn wraps around the base of the slipped stitch on the right needle).

Row 2 (WS): *P1, slip 1 wyib; repeat from * until 10 (12) stitches remain on the left needle, move yarn to the front of the work between needle tips and turn (working yarn wraps around the base of the slipped stitch on the right needle).

Row 3 (RS): K1, *slip 1 wyif, k1; repeat from * until 9 (11) stitches remain on the left needle, move yarn to the front and turn.

Row 4 (WS): *Slip 1 wyib, p1; repeat from * until 9 (11) stitches remain on the left needle, move yarn to the back and turn.

Row 5 (RS): Slip 1 wyif, *k1, slip 1 wyif; repeat from * until 8 (10) stitches remain on left needle, move yarn to the back of work and turn.

Continue working in the manner established in rows 2–5 until 1 stitch remains unworked at each end of the needle. End having worked a row 4.

Next row (RS): *Slip 1 wyif, k1; repeat from * to the last stitch on the needle, slip 1 wyif, move yarn to the back and turn.

Next row (WS): Ktbl, *slip 1 wyib, p1; repeat from * to the last stitch on the needle, slip 1 wyif, turn.

Gussets

With the right side facing, return to working in the round, as follows: *Switch to the smaller needles* and knit to the end of the heel stitches, place marker, pick up and knit 18 stitches along the edge of the sole flap. Using the instep needle, knit to the end of the instep stitches. With the small heel needle, pick up and knit 18 stitches along the other edge of the sole flap. Place marker to indicate a new beginning of round at the right edge of the heel—100 (104) stitches total.

Continue working in the round as follows:

Round 1: *Slip 1 wyib, k1; repeat from * to marker; slip marker, knit to the last 2 stitches on the heel needle, k2tog. Knit across all stitches on the instep needle. On the heel needle, ssk, knit to end-of-round marker.

Round 2: Knit.

Round 3: *K1, slip 1 wyib; repeat from * to marker; slip marker, knit to the last 2 stitches on the heel needle,

k2tog. Knit across all stitches on the instep needle. On the heel needle, ssk, knit to the end-of-round marker.

Round 4: Knit.

Repeat these 4 rounds until 1 stitch remains outside of the markers on the heel needle; end having worked a round 1.

Next round: Knit, removing both markers.

Next round: *K1, slip 1 wyib; repeat from * to the last 2 stitches on the heel needle, k2tog. Knit across all stitches on the instep needle. On the heel needle, ssk, knit to the end of the needle. Place marker to indicate a new end of round—64 (68) stitches total.

Leg

Work in stockinette stitch until the leg of the sock measures about 4 (5)" (10 [12.5]cm) from the top of the gusset, or 1" (2.5cm) less than the desired length.

Cuff

Round 1: *K1, p1; repeat from * to the end of the round.

Round 2: *K1, slip 1 wyif; repeat from * to the end of the round.

Repeat these 2 rounds until the cuff measures 1" (2.5cm).

Bind off very loosely using a traditional bind-off or Jeny's Surprisingly Stretchy Bind-Off (see page 187). Weave in ends.

Repeat the pattern to make a matching pair.

Annapurna

Designed by Ann Budd

Ann Budd knits socks the way I make tea—with alarming frequency (but with far more skill). She once joked that she never even really worried about durability, since a worn-out sock was just a welcome excuse to knit a new pair. Still, she was intrigued by the concept of creating a pair of indestructible socks. I asked her to design a rugged sock that would survive day after day of mountain trekking. As a play on the mountain-climbing idea and her own name, I named these socks Annapurna.

The socks use a soft but durable three-ply yarn made from Bluefaced Leicester wool, which tends to have a longer staple than Merino and, thus, greater resistance to abrasion. The leg and instep are worked in the two-row slip-stitch pattern commonly used to add strength to heel flaps. The last inch or so (2.5–3cm) of the heel flap, the heel turn, and the toe are all worked with two strands of yarn held together. The sole of the foot is also worked with two strands of yarn in a technique Mary Snyder used for her Padded Footlets in Favorite Socks. *Be sure to use a yarn with plenty of elasticity to compensate for the lack of true ribbing.*

The combination of slipped stitches and double strands on the heel make this sock an interesting option for variegated, semisolid, and solid yarns alike. Even if you don't plan to climb mountains, you'll find these socks extremely comfortable and warm.

SIZE
Women's S (M)

FINISHED MEASUREMENTS
Foot circumference: 6¾ (7½)" (17 [19]cm) unstretched, to fit foot circumference of about 7¾ (8½)" (19.5 [21.5]cm)

YARN
415 (535) yd (379 [489]m) of fingering-weight yarn: 1–2 (2) skeins String Theory Blue Stocking, 80% Bluefaced Leicester superwash, 20% nylon, 4 oz (113g), 420 yd (384m), color Jade

SUPER FINE

NEEDLES
Set of 4 U.S. size 1½ (2.5mm) double-pointed needles, or size to obtain gauge
Set of 4 U.S. size 2 (2.75mm) double-pointed needles, or 1 size larger than needles used to obtain gauge

NOTIONS
Tapestry needle

GAUGE
42 stitches and 60 rows = 4" (10cm) in slip-stitch pattern on smaller needles (worked in the round)

Notes

▸ *The lower part of the heel flap, the heel turn, and the toe are worked with 2 strands of yarn held together. The instep and gussets are worked with 1 strand of yarn, while the sole is worked alternately with 2 strands and then back and forth with 1 strand only (more details in the Foot section).*

▸ *The pattern is worked with 2 strands of yarn for most of the sock. If you are working with only 1 skein of yarn, the easiest solution is to wind your yarn into a center-pull ball and use the other end for the second strand.*

▸ *On the sole of the sock, when dropping the second strand of yarn to work with only 1 strand, do not cut the dropped strand.*

▸ *The larger needles are used only for the upper leg; the smaller needles are used for the remainder of each sock.*

▸ *Slipped stitches are slipped as if to purl, with the yarn held to the wrong side of the work.*

Stitch Guide

Slip-Stitch Pattern
Round 1: *Slip 1, k1; repeat from *.
Round 2: Knit.

Cuff
With larger needles, loosely cast on 72 (80) stitches. Divide stitches among 3 double-pointed needles and join to work in the round, being careful not to twist the stitches around the needles.
Rounds 1–8: *K1, p1; repeat from * to the end of the round.

Leg
Work in the Slip-Stitch Pattern on all stitches until the piece measures about 3½" (9cm) from the cast-on edge, ending with round 2 of the pattern.
Switch to smaller needles and continue working in the Slip-Stitch Pattern until the piece measures about 7 (7½)" (18 [19]cm) from the cast-on edge or until the desired leg length has been reached. End having

worked round 2 of the pattern.

Heel Flap
Rearrange the stitches as follows: Place the last 16 (18) stitches of the round on an empty needle. Using this same needle, work the next 16 (18) stitches in pattern as established. These 32 (36) stitches will be worked for the heel. Divide the remaining 40 (44) stitches evenly on 2 needles and hold them aside to be worked later for the instep.

Turn work to the wrong side and work the heel stitches back and forth in rows as follows:
Row 1 (WS): Slip 1, purl to the end of the needle. Turn work.
Row 2 (RS): *Slip 1, k1; repeat from * to the end of the needle. Turn.
Repeat these 2 rows until a total of 19 (21) rows have been worked, ending with a wrong-side row.
Continue in pattern to the center of the next right-side row, then add a second strand of yarn and continue in pattern as established with the yarn doubled for 18 (20) more rows. End having worked a wrong-side row.

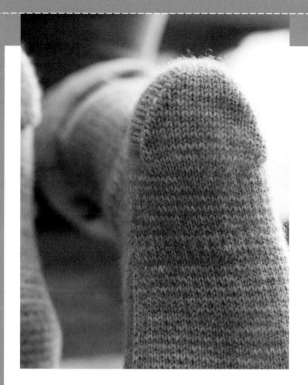

Turn Heel

Continue working in rows with the doubled yarn as follows:

Row 1 (RS): K18 (20), ssk, k1. Turn work.

Row 2 (WS): Slip 1, p5, p2tog, p1. Turn.

Row 3 (RS): Slip 1, knit to 1 stitch before the gap formed by the turn on the previous row, ssk (using 1 stitch on each side of the gap), k1. Turn.

Row 4 (WS): Slip 1, purl to 1 stitch before the gap formed by the turn on the previous row, p2tog (using 1 stitch on each side of the gap), p1. Turn.

Repeat rows 3 and 4 until all the heel stitches have been worked, omitting the final k1 on the last repeat of row 3 and omitting the final p1 on the last repeat of row 4—18 (20) heel stitches remain.

Gussets

The foot of this sock is worked in the round as follows: The instep and gussets are worked with 1 strand of yarn

only. The sole is worked with a doubled strand of yarn and then back and forth in 2 passes with a single strand of yarn. The sole stitches are worked 3 times for every 2 times the instep and gusset stitches are worked.

Round 1: With the right side facing and continuing with yarn doubled, slip 1, k17 (19) to the end of the heel stitches, then pick up and knit 1 stitch in each of the first 9 (10) selvedge stitches along the edge of the heel flap. Drop 1 strand of yarn to the wrong side of the work. With a second needle and a single strand of yarn, pick up and knit 1 stitch in each of the remaining 9 (10) selvedge stitches, pick up and knit 1 stitch at the base of the heel flap, then work the first 20 (22) instep stitches according to round 1 of the Slip-Stitch Pattern. With a third needle, work the remaining 20 (22) instep stitches in the Slip-Stitch Pattern, pick up and knit 1 stitch at the base of the heel flap, pick up and knit 1 stitch in each of the 18 (20) selvedge stitches, then transfer the last 8 (9) picked-up stitches from this needle onto the beginning of needle 1—96 (106) stitches total, with 35 (39) stitches on needle 1 (the sole needle), 30 (33) stitches on needle 2, and 31 (34) stitches on needle 3.

The working yarn is between the eighth and ninth (ninth and tenth) stitches of the sole needle; the other strand is at the end of the sole needle. Note that the first 8 (9) stitches on the sole needle are single stitches, not double as are the rest of the sole stitches. Rounds now begin at the beginning of the sole needle.

Round 2: Work the sole in 2 passes, then work the gusset and instep stitches, as follows:

> **Sole (RS):** Break the working yarn and rejoin it at the beginning of the sole needle, then k1, *slip 1, k1; repeat from * to end of the sole needle. Drop the working yarn to the wrong side and turn work.

> **Sole (WS):** Pick up the yarn dropped on the previous round, *slip 1, p1; repeat from * to the last stitch on

the sole needle, slip 1. Drop the working yarn to the wrong side and turn work.

Instep (RS): Skip to the end of the sole needle (do not work the sole stitches), pick up the single strand of yarn dropped there, and work the stitches on needles 2 and 3 as follows: Ssk, k57 (63) to the last 2 stitches on the needle 3, k2tog—2 gusset stitches decreased. Do not turn.

Both strands of yarn are at the beginning of the sole needle.

Round 3 (RS only): Holding both strands of yarn together and pulling tightly to remove the slack between them, knit to the end of the sole needle, drop 1 strand of yarn to the wrong side (do not turn). Continuing with 1 strand only, work across needles 2 and 3 as follows: K1, work in the Slip-Stitch Pattern as established to the last stitch on needle 3, k1. (For the first repeat of round 3, the Slip-Stitch Pattern will begin with a slip 1 for the small size and a knit 1 for the medium. This will alternate with each repeat of round 3.)

Round 4:

Sole (RS): Using the same single strand of yarn, k1, *slip 1, k1; repeat from * to the end of the sole needle, drop yarn to the wrong side. Turn.

Sole (WS): Pick up the strand dropped on the previous round, *slip 1, p1; repeat from * to the last stitch on the sole needle, slip 1, drop yarn to the wrong side. Turn.

Instep (RS): Skip to the end of the sole needle, pick up the single strand of yarn dropped there, and continue on to needles 2 and 3 as follows: Ssk, knit to last 2 stitches of needle 3, k2tog—2 gusset stitches decreased. Do not turn.

Both strands of yarn are at the beginning of the sole stitches.

Repeat rounds 3 and 4 until 37 (41) total stitches remain on needles 2 and 3—72 (80) stitches total.

Foot

Round 1 (RS only): Using both strands of yarn, knit to the end of the sole needle, drop 1 strand of yarn to the wrong side. Continuing with 1 strand only, work across needles 2 and 3 as follows: K1, work in the Slip-Stitch Pattern as established to the last stitch on needle 3, k1.

Round 2:

Sole (RS): Using the same single strand of yarn, k1, *slip 1, k1; repeat from * to the end of the sole needle, drop yarn to the wrong side. Turn.

Sole (WS): Pick up the strand dropped on the previous round, *slip 1, p1; repeat from * to the last stitch on the sole needle, slip 1, drop yarn to the wrong side. Turn.

Instep (RS): Skip to the end of the sole needle, pick up the single strand of yarn dropped there, and knit all

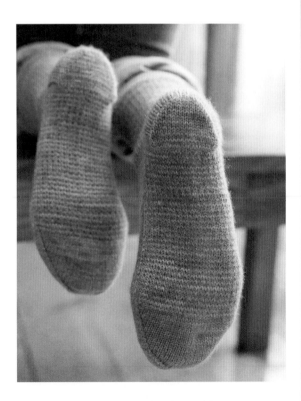

stitches on needles 2 and 3. Do not turn.

Both strands of yarn are at the beginning of the sole stitches.

Repeat the last 2 rounds until the foot measures 2 (2¼)" (5 [6]cm) less than the desired sock length, ending with a round 2.

Toe

Rearrange the stitches as follows: Move the first stitch on needle 2 to the end of needle 1 (sole needle), move the first stitch on needle 3 to the end of needle 2—36 (40) stitches on needle 1, and 18 (20) stitches on each of needles 2 and 3.

Work in the round with both strands held together, as follows:

Round 1: On needle 1, k1, ssk, knit to the last 3 stitches, k2tog, k1. On needle 2, k1, ssk, knit to the end of the needle. On needle 3, knit to the last 3 stitches, k2tog, k1.

Round 2: Knit all stitches.

Repeat the last 2 rounds until 40 total stitches remain, then repeat only round 1 until 16 total stitches remain. Move the stitches on needle 2 onto needle 3 and graft the toe closed with Kitchener stitch.

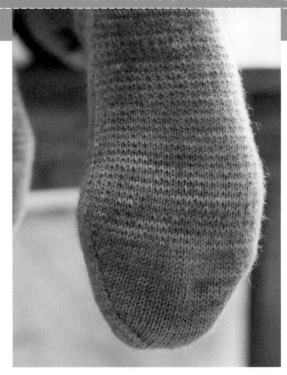

Weave in ends, tightening holes and loose stitches at gussets, if necessary.

Repeat the pattern to make a matching pair.

Caring for Socks

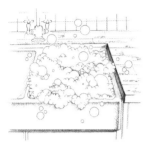

Maybe it's the New Englander in me, but I don't think a house is a home until there's a pair of socks drying next to the sink—or the fireplace, if you have one. I'm always baffled by the notion that a machine can wash clothes more efficiently than our hands. True, machines can use scalding hot water to thrash our Sunday finest far longer than our fingers could endure. But do handknitted socks require such vigorous treatment to get clean?

If your feet harbor highly infectious fungi, or if you spend your days in a coal mine, up a tree, or on a soccer field, you probably do want to let a washing machine do the work for you. For the rest of us, the process of washing socks by hand is a relaxing and pleasurable experience that uses far less energy than the kind that's delivered by a tube or wire, and it helps our lovely handiwork last a long, long time.

It's really quite simple. These instructions assume that your socks are made from a good, basic sock yarn, regardless of fiber content. I'd only be cautious if your socks were made from, say, potato starch or they were dyed using water-soluble ink—in which case you're on your own. Otherwise, follow these steps and you'll be fine.

First, fill a sink with warm water. How warm? If you get the water to around 100 to 110 degrees Fahrenheit (38–43° Celsius), it will be warm enough to dissolve most residues without damaging the fibers or weakening the dye saturation. Raw wool can handle hotter water, but once the yarn has been dyed and knit, you want to be careful with hotter temperatures until you know the yarn better. Hot water can make some yarns felt or stretch, or cause their colors to bleed or fade. Always test a knitted swatch first.

Next, dissolve some soap into the water, giving it a good slosh to make sure it's evenly distributed. Socks can get a tad dirtier than your average scarf or cardigan, so you'll want to add a soap that gives you a sense of doing the job. I've had fine results with Eucalan, Soak, Kookaburra, or Unicorn Fibre Wash. In a pinch, I often use a gentle shampoo or dishwashing liquid, such as Dawn or Ivory.

My major concern with washing socks in the machine isn't as much about the machine itself but the detergent we usually toss into the wash. You'll get a far longer, more vibrant, and pleasantly tactile life out of your handknitted socks if you use a gentler soap, such as the ones I've just mentioned. Standard laundry detergents often have harsher enzymes and bleaching agents that are useful for washing towels and jeans but can gradually suck all the liveliness out of your wool-based handknitted socks.

Now that you've filled your sink and added a mild soap, drop your socks into the water and give them a few gentle taps and squeezes to make sure the water has penetrated all the nooks and crannies. Then let your socks rest for thirty minutes to an hour. Make a cup of tea, answer e-mails, or just leave your hands in the hot water, gaze out a window, and think deep thoughts.

Once that time has passed, return to the sink and give your socks a few more tender squeezes. You want to circulate the warm soapy water one more time to remove any residue that has come loose during the soak.

Then squeeze the socks together and lift them from the water. Set them aside and refill the sink with water warm of the same temperature. (Protein fibers don't like surprises of the hot-to-cold variety; if your socks are made from non-machine-washable wool, they may felt slightly from the shock.) Drop the socks back in, swirling and squishing again to circulate the new clean water throughout all the fibers and stitches. Unless your socks were particularly dirty or the rinse water is still murky, you'll only need to rinse once. Additional rinses don't do any damage, so if you're nervous, go ahead and repeat the rinsing process until you're satisfied.

At this point, lay the socks out on a towel, roll them up, and squeeze the towel several times to remove excess water.

Now you have a choice. You can slip your socks onto a sock blocker and let them dry to shape. If you do this, they'll dry quite flat and smooth in the shape of a sock that's been squished sideways by a steamroller. This technique can leave a crease along the top of the instep, but that crease tends to disappear in a snug-fitting sock. You can also leave the socks on the towel and let them dry as is, again letting the negative ease smooth everything out on your foot. Or you can do as Cat Bordhi and others do, slipping the socks onto your own foot after you've blotted them dry in a towel. Squeeze, tap, and nudge the sock on your foot until the sock fits perfectly, then gently slide the sock off your foot and set it back on the towel to dry in perfect shape. All these methods work just fine.

Last but not least, take out your favorite hand lotion and apply it liberally to your hands, giving them a good massage. You deserve it.

Abbreviations and Techniques

Backward-Loop Cast-On: Using the working yarn, make a backward loop and place it on the right-hand needle so that the working yarn points toward you. Repeat until you have cast on the desired number of stitches.

Double-Start Cast-On: This method involves casting on 1 stitch with the traditional long-tail cast-on and then casting on 1 stitch with a modified method. To begin, follow the instructions for the long-tail cast-on (see page 188) to put a slipknot on the needle and cast on 1 stitch.

Then, keeping your hands in the same position, move your left thumb out and away from between the hanging strands of yarn, and wrap it around the yarn from the opposite direction. Now move the tip of the needle straight down between your thumb and index finger and lift the strand near your palm (the strand that runs from behind your thumb to your three other fingers).

Then move the needle over the strand around your index finger, bring it back through the loop on the thumb, and drop the loop off your thumb. Place your thumb back in the position for the long-tail cast-on and tighten up the stitch you just cast on.

Continue in this manner, casting on 1 stitch with the long-tail cast-on and 1 stitch as just described, until you have the desired number of stitches on the needle.

You can watch Nancy Bush demonstrate this cast-on in the *Knitting Daily* TV Episode 212 excerpt here: http://www.youtube.com/watch?v=Frc5_9AIVy0.

Elizabeth Zimmermann's Sewn Bind-Off: This is a wonderful technique for creating an elastic bind-off edge. Cut yarn, leaving a tail about 4 times as long as the edge you're binding off. Thread the yarn tail onto a tapestry needle. *Insert the tapestry needle through the first 2 stitches as if to purl them together; pull the yarn through, but leave both stitches on the left-hand needle. Then insert the tapestry needle through the first stitch as if to knit it, pull the yarn through, and slip that stitch off the left-hand needle. Repeat from * until 1 stitch remains on the left-hand needle, insert tapestry needle through that stitch purlwise, pull the yarn through, and slip the stitch off the needle.

Jeny's Surprisingly Stretchy Bind-Off: Popularized by Jeny Staiman, this clever bind-off is similar to the standard bind-off, but with a yarn-over worked before each stitch. It is worked as follows: If your first stitch is a knit, make a reverse yarn-over (wrapping the yarn from the back, over the right-hand needle, and between the needles to the back again), then knit the stitch. If your first stitch is a purl, make a normal yarn-over, then purl the stitch. Pass the yarn-over over the stitch just worked. *If the next stitch is a knit, make a reverse yarn-over and k1; if the next stitch is a purl, yo and p1. Pass the rightmost 2 stitches on the right-hand needle (the k or p and the yo) over the stitch just worked. Repeat from * until 1 stitch remains on the right-hand needle. Cut the yarn and pull the last loop.

Judy's Magic Cast-On: Developed by Judy Becker, this technique creates a completely invisible cast-on that's perfect for toe-up socks. The best way to learn Judy's Magic Cast-On is by watching someone else work it. You'll see that it's far more easy and intuitive than words alone could convey here. Judy offers an excellent written tutorial on her Web site, www.persistentillusion.com. Cat Bordhi provides a very clear and helpful tutorial on YouTube. This tutorial, which can be viewed at http://www.youtube.com/watch?v=IhBISOAhhQY (or by going to YouTube.com and searching for "Cat Bordhi magic cast-on"), shows the new, modified cast-on in which the stitches are not twisted on the second needle. All the patterns in this book use the newer, modified cast-on.

K: Knit.

K2tog: Knit 2 stitches together.

K3tog: Knit 3 stitches together.

Kfb (knit front and back): Knit through the front loop of the next stitch but do not take it off the left-hand needle; knit through the back loop of the same stitch, then slip both stitches off the left-hand needle.

Kitchener stitch: Arrange your stitches on 2 needles so that the needle closest to you contains the first half of the stitches to be joined and the needle farthest from you contains the second half of the stitches, with the yarn tail coming out of the right side of the far needle. Thread the tail through a darning needle.

Pass the darning needle through the fist stitch on the front needle from right to left, as if you were going to purl that stitch. Next, run your darning needle through the first stitch on the back needle from left to right, as if you were going to knit it.

Each time you move from the front needle to back, make sure the yarn passes around the right side of the needles and not over them.

Now, pass the darning needle through the first stitch on your front needle as if to knit it, and let the stitch slide off your needle. Then pass your darning needle through the next stitch on the front needle as if to purl. Thread the darning needle through the first stitch on your back needle as if to purl, and let that stitch slide off the needle. Now

thread the darning needle through the next stitch on the back needle as if to knit.

Repeat the last few steps as follows: Enter the first stitch on the front needle as if to knit, remove that stitch, and enter the next stitch as if to purl. Then on the back needle, enter the first stitch as if to purl, remove that stitch, and enter the next stitch as if to knit. Proceed in this fashion, alternately working 2 stitches on the front needle and then 2 stitches on the back needle, removing a stitch after it has been worked twice.

When 1 stitch remains on each needle, run the darning needle knitwise through the stitch on the front needle and let it slip off the needle, then slip the darning needle purlwise through the final stitch on the back needle and let it slip off.

Knitwise: As if to knit.

Ktbl: Knit through the back loop of the stitch (twisting the stitch).

Lli (left-lifted increase): Insert the tip of the left needle from front to back into the left leg of the stitch that is 2 stitches below the stitch you just worked on the right-hand needle. Raise this stitch onto the left-hand needle and knit it.

Long-Tail Cast-On: The success of the long-tail cast-on depends on the tail being truly long enough to accommodate all the stitches you need to cast on. To get a general idea of how much yarn you need per stitch, wrap the yarn around your needle once and measure it. Multiply this times the number of stitches you're casting on, add a few inches (several cm) for good measure, and you'll be set.

Create a slipknot at the end of the above-mentioned long

tail. Place this slipknot on a needle and hold it in your right hand so that the tail hangs closest to you. With your left hand, poke your thumb and index finger toward you between the 2 hanging strands of yarn, grab them with your other fingers so that they are secured on the palm of your left hand, and then twist your hand backward while opening up your thumb and index finger so that they make a V. The yarn is wrapped around each finger in the right position for your next step.

Insert the tip of your needle through the bottom of the loop on your thumb and draw it upward. With that yarn still on the needle, hook the needle over the top and around the back of the loop on your index finger, and bring the needle back through the loop on your thumb. While keeping the strands secured in the palm of your hand, let your thumb slip out of the loop and pull the tail gently to tighten the newly formed stitch on your needle. Then move your fingers back into the original V position and continue casting on this way until you've reached the desired number of stitches.

M1 (backward-loop make 1): Using the working yarn, make a backward loop and place it on the right-hand needle so that the working yarn points toward you.

M1 (make 1): Pick up the bar between the stitches from front to back, and knit into the back of the picked-up stitch.

M1L (make 1 left): Make a left-leaning increase by picking up the bar between stitches from front to back and knitting into the back of the picked-up stitch.

M1R (make 1 right): Make a right-leaning increase by picking up the bar between stitches from back to front and knitting into the front of the picked-up stitch.

P: Purl.

P2tog: Purl 2 stitches together.

P3tog: Purl 3 stitches together.

Provisional Cast-On: Use this cast-on when you will want to access your cast-on stitches later (e.g., to create a hemmed cuff on a pair of socks). My favorite provisional cast-on is a crochet provisional cast-on, which comes to us from Lucy Neatby (who walks you through it in her *Knitting Essentials 2 DVD*).

Take a knitting needle that's the size required for your project, plus a crochet hook and a length of scrap yarn that's the same thickness as your project yarn but, ideally, in a different color so you can see it clearly. Be sure you have enough yarn to cast on all the stitches required.

Using the scrap yarn, create a slipknot on the crochet hook, and hold the crochet hook in your right hand. Place the knitting needle to the left of the crochet hook so that they are parallel to each other, with the working yarn running from the crochet hook and behind the knitting needle, and held in your left hand. With the crochet hook, reach over the top of your knitting needle and wrap the yarn around the hook, then pull it through the slipknot. You have now created 1 stitch on the knitting needle.

Before you can repeat this step, you'll need to move your working yarn around your knitting needle and to the back again. Now you're ready to reach the crochet hook over the top of the knitting needle, wrap the yarn around the hook again, and pull it through the loop on your hook.

When your total number of desired stitches is on the knitting needle, make an emergency crochet chain with a few more stitches, just using the crochet hook and not catching the stitches around the knitting needle. Your provisional cast-on is now complete. When you're ready to unravel your provisional cast-on, simply find the emergency crochet chain and tug the end to unravel the whole chain and release those cast-on stitches.

Ptbl: Purl through the back loop of the stitch (twisting the stitch).

Purlwise: As if to purl.

Rli (right-lifted increase): Insert the tip of the right-hand needle from front to back into the right leg of the stitch below the next stitch on the left-hand needle. Raise this stitch onto the left-hand needle and knit it.

RS (right side): Generally, the side of the garment that will face away from the skin when it is worn; the "public" side.

Slip 1 (or slip 1 purlwise): Slide 1 stitch from the left-hand needle to the right-hand needle without working or twisting it in any way.

Slip 1 knitwise (or slip 1 as if to knit): Slide 1 stitch from the left-hand needle to the right-hand needle as if to knit, but without working it.

Ssk (slip, slip, knit): Slip 1 stitch as if to knit, slip another stitch as if to knit, replace both stitches on the left-hand needle, and then knit them together through the back loops.

Ssp (slip, slip, purl): Slip 1 stitch as if to knit, slip another stitch as if to knit, replace both stitches on the left-hand needle, and then purl them together through the back loops.

Three-Needle Bind-Off: Arrange the stitches to be joined on 2 needles. Hold both needles parallel in the left hand, with the right sides together, unless your pattern specifies otherwise. Insert a third, working needle through the first stitch on the front needle, then through the first stitch on the back needle; knit these stitches together. Repeat, and then pass the first new stitch over the stitch just made and off the right-hand needle. Continue in this manner, knitting together 1 stitch from each needle and then binding them off as you go.

Working wrapped stitches: When knitting a wrap together with its stitch, turn the wrapped stitch by slipping it as if to knit and then returning it to the left-hand needle. Insert the tip of the right-hand needle under the near side of the wrap and lift it onto the left-hand needle. Then knit the wrap and the stitch together.

When purling a wrap together with its stitch, insert the tip of the right-hand needle under the far side of the wrap and lift it onto the left-hand needle. Then purl together the wrap and the stitch.

W&T (wrap and turn): With yarn to the wrong side of the work, slip the next stitch purlwise. Bring yarn to the right side of the work and move the slipped stitch back onto the left-hand needle. Turn work, ready to knit or purl in the other direction.

WS (wrong side): Generally the side that will face toward the skin when the garment is worn; the "private" side.

Yo (yarn-over): Wrap the yarn around the right-hand needle in the same manner that you would wrap it while knitting a stitch—only do so without touching any stitches on your left-hand needle.

Foot Length Tables

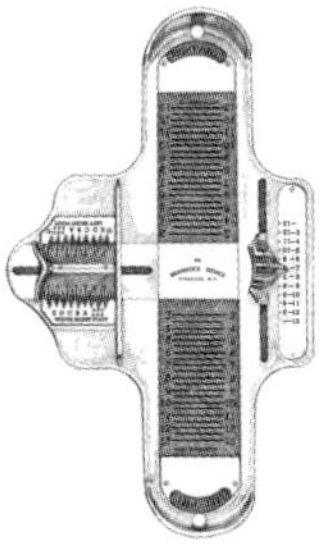

As you probably know from your own shoe-shopping experience, no absolute size standard exists among shoe manufacturers. A U.S. size 8 from one maker may be noticeably smaller than a size 8 from a different manufacturer. And don't forget that your own feet may not even match each other in length.

Still, knowing the *average* foot length for a particular shoe size allows you to knit socks for a friend or loved one without having to measure that person's foot. The following charts give the average foot lengths for a number of shoe manufacturers. Use it as a general guide, knowing that there could be as much as ¼" (6mm) of variation in either direction.

Also remember to plan for negative ease. As I mentioned in chapter 4, you'll want to maintain a negative ease of at least 10 percent in your sock, meaning that you'll want the sock to be 10 percent smaller than your foot—both in terms of leg circumference and overall sock length. At an absolute bare minimum, the sock should be ⅓" (8.5mm) shorter than the desired sock length.

WOMEN'S SHOE SIZES

U.S.	UK	EURO	INCHES/CM
5	3	35–36	8 ½"/21.6cm
5½	3½	36	8¾"/22.2cm
6	4	36–37	8 9/11"/22.4cm
6½	4½	37	9"/23cm
7	5	37–38	9¼"/23.5cm
7½	3½	38	9⅜"/23.8cm
8	6	38–39	9½"/24cm
8½	6½	39	9 11/16"/24.6cm
9	7	39–40	9⅞"/25.1cm
9½	7½	40	10"/25.4cm
10	8	40–41	10 3/16"/25.9cm
10½	8½	41	10 5/16"/26.2cm
11	9	41–42	10½"/26.7cm
11½	9½	42	10 11/16"/27cm
12	10	42–43	10 7/10"/27.2cm

MEN'S SHOE SIZES

U.S.	UK	EURO	INCHES/CM
6	5½	39	9¼"/23.5cm
6½	6	39	9½"/24cm
7	6½	40	9⅝"/24.4cm
7½	7	40–41	9¾"/24.8cm
8	7½	41	$9\frac{15}{16}$"/25.2cm
8½	8	41–42	10⅛"/25.7cm
9	8½	42	10¼"/26cm
9½	9	42–43	$10\frac{7}{16}$"/26.5cm
10	9½	43	$10\frac{9}{16}$"/26.8cm
10½	10	43–44	10¾"/27.3cm
11	10½	44	$10\frac{15}{16}$"/27.8cm
11½	11	44–45	11⅛"/28.3cm
12	11½	45	11¼"/28.6cm
13	12½	46	$11\frac{9}{16}$"/29.4cm
14	13½	47	$11\frac{7}{10}$"/29.7cm
15	14½	48	$12\frac{3}{16}$"/31cm
16	15½	49	12½"/31.8cm

CHILDREN'S SHOE SIZES

U.S.	UK	EURO	INCHES/CM
6	5	22	5⅛"/13cm
7	6	23	5½"/14cm
8	7	24	5¾"/14.6cm
9	8	25	6⅛"/15.6cm
10	9	27	6½"/16.5cm
11	10	28	6¾"/17.1cm
12	11	30	7⅛"/18cm
13	12	31	7½"/19cm
1	13	32	7¾"/19.7cm
2	1	33	8⅛"/20.6cm
3	2	34	8½"/21.6cm
4	3	36	8¾"/22.2cm
5	4	37	9⅛"/23.2cm
6	5	38	9½"/24.1cm
7	6	39	9¾"/24.8cm

Materials Resources

ALCHEMY YARNS OF TRANSFORMATION

www.alchemyyarns.com

AUSTERMANN, *distributed in the United States by Skacel*

www.skacelknitting.com

BERROCO

www.berroco.com

BIJOU BASIN RANCH

www.bijoubasinranch.com

BLACK BUNNY FIBERS

www.blackbunnyfibers.com

BLUE MOON FIBER ARTS

www.bluemoonfiberarts.com

BROOKLYN TWEED

www.brooklyntweed.net

CLASSIC ELITE YARNS

www.classiceliteyarns.com

EUCALAN

www.eucalan.com

HILL TRIBE

(silver leaf charms in Sivia Harding's Lady Tryamour)

www.artbeads.com

KATHRYN ALEXANDER DESIGNS

www.kathrynalexander.net

KOOKABURRA WOOLWASH

www.kookaburraco.com

LANG YARNS, *distributed in the United States by Berroco*

www.berroco.com

LORNA'S LACES

www.lornaslaces.net

LOUET NORTH AMERICA

www.louet.com

LUCY NEATBY CAT'S PAJAMAS

www.lucyneatby.com

MADELINETOSH

www.madelinetosh.com

MALABRIGO YARN

www.malabrigoyarn.com

MOUNTAIN COLORS YARNS

www.mountaincolors.com

NORO, *distributed in the United States by Knitting Fever*

www.knittingfever.com

ONLINE, *distributed in the United States by Knitting Fever*

www.knittingfever.com

QUINCE & CO.

www.quinceandco.com

SCHOPPEL WOLLE, *distributed in the United States by Skacel*
www.skacelknitting.com

SHIBUI KNITS
www.shibuiknits.com

SOAK WASH
www.soakwash.com

SPIRIT TRAIL FIBERWORKS
www.spirit-trail.net

STRING THEORY
www.stringtheoryyarn.com

SUNDARA YARN
www.sundarayarn.com

SWANS ISLAND YARNS
www.swansislandblankets.com

UNICORN FIBRE WASH
www.unicornfibre.com

A VERB FOR KEEPING WARM
www.averbforkeepingwarm.com

ZITRON, *distributed in the United States by Skacel*
www.skacelknitting.com

Craft Yarn Council Standard Yarn Weight System

YARN WEIGHT SYMBOL AND CATEGORY NAMES	0 LACE	1 SUPER FINE	2 FINE	3 LIGHT	4 MEDIUM	5 BULKY	6 SUPER BULKY
TYPE OF YARNS IN CATEGORY	Fingering 10-count crochet thread	Sock, Fingering, Baby	Sport, Baby	DK, Light Worsted	Worsted, Afghan, Aran	Chunky, Craft, Rug	Bulky, Roving
KNIT GAUGE RANGE* IN STOCKINETTE TO 4"	33–40**sts	27–32 sts	23–26 sts	21–24 sts	16–20 sts	12–15 sts	6–11 sts
RECOMMENDED NEEDLE SIZE, METRIC	1.5–2.25mm	2.25–3.25mm	3.25–3.75mm	3.75–4.5mm	4.5–5.5mm	5.5–8mm	8mm and larger
RECOMMENDED NEEDLE SIZE, U.S.	000–1	1–3	3–5	5–7	7–9	9–11	11 and larger

* Please note that these are GUIDELINES ONLY based on the most commonly used gauges and needle or hook sizes for specific yarn categories.

** Lace-weight yarns are usually worked on larger needles to create lacy, openwork patterns. Accordingly, a gauge range is difficult to determine. Always follow the gauge stated in your pattern.

Recommended Reading

An abundance of books and videos exist to guide you on your sock-knitting journey. Many of them were created by the designers featured in this book—and I've included them here because they truly are leaders in their field.

If you're just getting started knitting socks, Ann Budd wrote a clear and helpful book with this very same title—*Getting Started Knitting Socks*. Intended for absolute beginners, Ann walks you through your very first cast-on all the way to a perfect Kitchener-stitch ending.

While the rest of the world seems to operate on one standard system of gravity, the sock-knitting world has two: socks knit from the top down and those knit from the toe up. For a wealth of top-down sock design inspiration, check out Cookie A's *Sock Innovation* and *Knit. Sock. Love.* If you're more of a toe-upper, get copies of Wendy D. Johnson's *Socks from the Toe Up* and *Toe-Up Socks for Every Body*. To explore toe-up socks further, Chrissy Gardiner's *Toe-Up!* is a vast and helpful master class on the subject—complete with many tempting patterns for feet of all sizes.

For those who prefer to be given the keys and let loose on their own road, Charline Schurch's *Sensational Knitted Socks* and *More Sensational Knitted Socks* fit the bill perfectly. Both books are structured around a "pick your motif" theme where you choose the yarn, gauge, and stitch, and simply plug it into a master pattern.

Visual learners, or those who simply enjoy a little company while they knit, will want to run out right now and get copies of Lucy Neatby's *A Knitter's Companion Sock Techniques 1 and 2* DVDs. The first DVD will get you up and running, while the second one will give you all sorts of brilliant tips that will leave you feeling quite clever. Many of the things shown in these DVDs are also included in her booklet,

Cool Socks Warm Feet, but they're even more enjoyable when explained in Lucy's own voice.

Speaking of voices, I urge you to pick up a copy of Elizabeth Zimmermann's *Knitting Around* for the sheer pleasure of hearing Elizabeth's voice as you knit. She guides you through her Moccasin Sock, whose ingenious and practical construction produces a sock whose foot is entirely reknittable.

Among contemporary sock thinkers, Cat Bordhi helped fuel the last decade of sock exploration with her *Socks Soar on Two Circular Needles* and *New Pathways for Sock Knitters: Book One*. Both books require a brief suspension of all your beliefs about how you think a sock could (or should) be constructed—but the rewards, and that "aha!" moment, are worth it.

Impatient knitters, or those simply afflicted with the dreaded Second Sock Syndrome, owe Melissa Morgan-Oakes a debt of gratitude. She first figured out a way to knit two socks at the same time on one very long circular needle, all of which is detailed in *2-at-a-Time Socks*. Then she turned the sock upside down and showed how you could use the same technique to knit socks from the toe up, as you'll read about in *Toe-Up 2-at-a-Time Socks*.

If you know you're ready to dig deeper into sock-knitting technique and history, two books stand out. The first is Nancy Bush's *Folk Socks*, a painstakingly researched and well-written ode to the tradition of knitted footwear around the world, complete with archival photographs and contemporary patterns. The second is *Vogue Knitting: The Ultimate Sock Book*, which pairs history with a broad survey of technique, pulling it all together with twenty-five sock patterns.

To challenge yourself and keep the inspiration fresh, consider joining a sock club. For a fee, every few months you'll receive a new pattern and yarn in the mail—and you'll be able to get support and encouragement online from your fellow club members. The mother of all sock clubs is the Rockin' Sock Club run by Tina Newton of Blue Moon

Fiber Arts. Every other month, you receive two patterns (one from a seasoned designer, and one from a relative newcomer) that are clearly written, thoroughly edited, and well-photographed, accompanied by yarn in a colorway conceived for the project—and, of course, there's the letter from Tina, which is always a pleasure to read.

Finally, consider visiting KnittersReview.com to sign up for my weekly e-mail newsletter. Every week, you'll learn about new, unusual, and otherwise noteworthy yarns, books, tools, and events that will make your sock-knitting experience even more pleasurable.

About the Designers

COOKIE A (PAGE 73)

Cookie A is the author of *Sock Innovation* and *Knit. Sock. Love*. Her patterns have been featured in various print and online periodicals. She teaches intensive sock design workshops internationally. Visit her Web site at cookiea.com.

KATHRYN ALEXANDER (PAGE 167)

Kathryn Alexander is an internationally known textile artist—a spinner, weaver, dyer, and knitter whose work is characterized by an abundance of color, richly textured surfaces, and whimsical designs. She and her work have been featured in several magazines, including *Fiberarts*, *Surface Design*, *Ornament*, *Spin-Off*, and *Interweave Knits*, as well as in a number of books. When not spinning, weaving, dyeing, and knitting, Kathryn can be found working in her flower and vegetable gardens or riding her horses through fields and woods that surround her small farm in upstate New York. See Kathryn's work on her Web site, kathrynalexander.net.

A. KAREN ALFKE (PAGE 173)

Karen has been designing her own garments since she first learned how to knit in Germany in the 1980s. She learned to knit and design at the hands of an amazingly talented intuitive designer, her aunt Anne (after whom she's named, hence the initial A in her name). Karen began developing her "Unpatterns" series in 1998 as a way to pass on the skills she learned from her aunt—and the first Unpattern was a sock. In addition to her Unpatterns pattern line, she also designs under the 2nd Nature Design label. When she's not teaching, she knits, designs, and pets her dog in Port Townsend, Washington.

MARLAINA BIRD (PAGE 95)

Crochet and knitwear designer Marlaina Bird actually learned to knit so that she could knit socks. Her first project was a pair in stockinette stitch using self-striping yarn. Socks hold a special place in heart because they're the one thing she makes that everybody in her family wants. Needless to say, it makes knitting socks as gifts superfun. Her patterns have been published in *Knitscene* and *Interweave Crochet*; she hosts a live podcast called *Yarn Thing* on Blog Talk Radio; and she blogs at www.knitthing.blogspot.com.

CAT BORDHI (PAGE 61)

Cat is gifted with a mind that's constantly solving puzzles before the rest of us even know the puzzle exists. She teaches and inspires more than 1,000 knitters each year in her classes all over North America. Her YouTube knitting tutorials have nearly one million views, and her innovative books, *Socks Soar on Two Circular Needles*, *A Treasury of Magical Knitting*, *A Second Treasury of Magical Knitting*, *New Pathways for Sock Knitters*, and *Personal Footprints for Insouciant Sock Knitters* have reached well over 100,000 knitters. She is also the author of an award-winning novel, *Treasure Forest*. For more information, visit catbordhi.com, or Cat's Facebook page.

ANN BUDD (PAGE 179)

The day Ann Budd put on her first handknitted sock, she fell in love all over again. She hasn't worn store-bought socks in six years. Ann is the bestselling author of a dozen knitting books, including *The Knitter's Handy Book of Patterns*, *The Knitter's Handy Book of Sweater Patterns*, *Getting Started Knitting Socks*, and *Sock Knitting Master Class: Innovative Techniques and Patterns from Top Designers*. Formerly the senior editor of *Interweave Knits* magazine, she is now a book editor and knitwear designer. Ann lives in Boulder, Colorado, and blogs at annbuddknits.com.

NANCY BUSH (PAGE 131)

Nancy Bush found her way to traditional knitting techniques and uses of ethnic patterns via a degree in art history and postgraduate studies in color design and weaving in San Francisco and Sweden. She has published articles and designs in *PieceWork*, *Knitter's*, *Interweave Knits*, *Spin-Off*, *Vogue Knitting*, and *Threads*. She teaches workshops in the United States and abroad and owns The Wooly West, a mail-order yarn business in Salt Lake City, Utah. She is the author of *Folk Socks*, *Folk Knitting in Estonia*, *Knitting on the Road*, *Knitting Vintage Socks*, and *Knitted Lace of Estonia: Techniques, Patterns, and Tradition*. She loves designing and knitting socks from the top down on DPNs, and she feels a connection to knitters of the past with every stitch.

JANE COCHRAN (PAGE 67)

Jane Cochran knits, spins, and runs a bookstore on the East End of Long Island, New York. Her favorite knitting project is a pair of socks in soft wool fingering-weight yarn, dyed in a beautiful shade of just about any color, and knit with 2.5mm double-pointed needles. In fact, she thinks that if perfection exists it might be found in that graceful little collapsible square built out of wooden sticks and knitted stitches. Jane blogs about knitting and navigating her world at not-plain-jane.com.

JARED FLOOD (PAGE 151)

Jared Flood is a New York–based designer and blogger. He's never been crazy about wearing knitting on his feet, but he has a special weakness for wooly house socks that can be worn in place of slippers. See more of his work at www.brooklyntweed.net.

NORAH GAUGHAN (PAGE 89)

A professional knitting designer for more than twenty years, Norah Gaughan has freelanced for major yarn companies and knitting magazines, designed pattern stitches for ready-to-wear, and been the design director for two major yarn companies. During a "hiatus" between design-director gigs, Norah wrote *Knitting Nature: 39 Designs Inspired by Patterns in Nature*. She is currently the design director at Berroco, where she helps provide hundreds of new knitting patterns for knitters each year. She recently coauthored *Comfort Knitting and Crochet: Afghans*, which features more than fifty designs for Berroco's Comfort yarn.

JENNIFER HAGAN (PAGE 85)

Jennifer Hagan's past includes being a professional vocalist and English teacher, but her present is all about being the mother of three, the Grammy of four, and the wife of one, Fred. Her designs have been published in most major knitting magazines and a nice list of books, and she's had a few crochet designs published as well. Jen has two pattern lines, Figheadh Yarnworks, which is wholesale, and Mirth Designs, which is available for purchase online. She most enjoys designing with cables and tries to sneak them in whenever possible—that is, when not preaching to people to block their projects. Jen has knit and/or designed just about every kind of sock, but her favorite socks to knit are toe-up, short-row heel, stockinette-stitch socks with hand-dyed yarn. Simple is best. Follow her exploits on her blog, http://figknits.blogspot.com.

ANNE HANSON (PAGE 101)

Designer, teacher, and Knitspot owner Anne Hanson is a lifelong knitter with a background in the fashion and graphic design fields. Early on, Anne had a cantankerous relationship with sock knitting. She found it largely boring, but she endured it for the sake of her brother, who is so fond of handknit socks. After falling in love with David, an enthusiastic sock (and yarn) appreciator, she found her muse and began to understand that handknit socks can be a powerful charm for a happy marriage. Since that time, she cannot be found without a sock on the needles and often has several designs in progress at once.

Anne's design work has been included in *Knitty*, *The Knitter*, *Interweave Knits*, and *Twist Collective*, as well as several upcoming publications. In addition, her designs have been commissioned for several popular sock and lace clubs, including the Rockin' Sock Club, the Woolgirl sock and lace clubs, the Yarn4Socks club, and the Fearless Fibers clubs. Anne lives and works in Ohio with David, who loves wool, too. She blogs at knitspot.com.

SIVIA HARDING (PAGE 123)

Sivia Harding was not born a sock knitter. After she learned how to knit in 2000, it took her a couple of years to make friends with knitting at a good sock gauge, and then a couple more to fall in love with the delightful possibilities of designing socks. She blames Cat Bordhi for pulling her down the rabbit hole with her ingenious designs and "sockitectures." A sucker for interesting shaping, Sivia also dabbles in lace and beads. She knits and designs from Portland, Oregon, and you can find her patterns for sale at siviaharding.com and at numerous yarn stores.

STEPHEN HOUGHTON (PAGE 77)

As a wee neophyte knitter, Stephen swore never to attempt socks, let alone any project that required needles smaller than U.S. 6 (4mm). Now, the proud owner of many decades' worth of sock yarn, he's placed his wool-clad foot in his mouth. (As an aspiring circus freak, he really is that flexible.) An equal-opportunity knitter, he'll start from toe or cuff and anywhere in between and gladly follow Cat Bordhi down any pathway she may wander. It was her *Socks Soar on Two Circular Needles* that convinced him to attempt his first pair. Socks also brought his mother back into the knitting fold after thirty-five-plus years away from the needles.

When he's not contemplating handsome hems, the joy of mismatched socks, and architectural construction techniques, he can be found in San Francisco making salted caramels (the candy, not the socks), baking bread for his photographer husband, and playing with his French bulldog, the elegantly butch Janie Sparkles.

MELISSA MORGAN-OAKES (PAGE 115)

Melissa Morgan-Oakes learned as a child to crochet, tat, and sew without commercial patterns. She later taught herself to spin and knit and so brings the perspective of a self-taught knitter to her innovative methods. Melissa revolutionized the world of sock knitting with the best-selling *2-at-a-Time Socks*. Her ingenious approach showed delighted knitters how to simultaneously create two socks on a single circular needle. When not plotting world sock domination, she lives, writes, and raises chickens in western Massachusetts with her family.

LUCY NEATBY (PAGE 155)

Formerly a British Merchant Navy navigating officer, Lucy is now a full-time knitting designer, writer, and teacher. She loves all types of knitting, as long as they feature exuberant colorwork. As a teacher she gets a kick out of empowering knitters to take control of their stitches. To spread her message she has filmed the sixteen-title *Learn with Lucy* DVD series and written two books: *Cool Socks Warm Feet* and *Cool Knitters Finish in Style*. Lucy's fascination with socks was cemented by the miracle of her first sock heel worked from a pattern. Ever since then, she has pursued the quest for the ultimate sock. This has resulted in socks worked from many different directions and featuring a wide variety of innovative techniques. Her current passion (or maybe obsession) is for double-layer knit fabrics, which here result in superwarm socks for you.

CIRILIA ROSE (PAGE 145)

Cirilia Rose knits and designs in the Northeast and is inspired by all things cinematic. When she isn't knitting in darkened theaters, she enjoys making messes in the kitchen and visiting friends who are scattered around the United States. Although she doesn't consider herself much of a sock knitter, that doesn't seem to stop her from collecting sock yarn. Maybe it is the thrift, or the beautifully inventive colorways, or perhaps it is her love for all things striped. Her yarn collection continues to outpace production.

SANDI ROSNER (PAGE 137)

Sandi Rosner knit her first pair of socks more than fifteen years ago, using double-stranded, worsted-weight yarn on U.S. size 8 (5mm) needles. She has knit many socks since then, and she's learned to love fingering-weight yarn and tiny double-pointed needles. Sandi is the author of *Not Just Socks*, *Not Just More Socks*, and *Not Just Socks for Kids*. She experienced total sock immersion while writing the patterns for *Think Outside the Sox*. A designer, tech editor, teacher, and writer who is never without a sock in progress ready for on-the-go knitting, Sandi lives in northern California.

JAYME STAHL (PAGE 107)

Jayme Stahl learned to knit at a young age from her grandmother. She rediscovered knitting in college, when she became an obsessed knitter, learning as many techniques as she could find and applying those to her own designs. A former software developer, she is currently staying at home as a full-time mother and knitwear designer. She designs, knits, and spins at her home in Virginia.

Acknowledgments

How ironic that I should write a book about socks. Growing up in sunny Arizona and summering in coastal Maine, sandals and flip-flops were the norm. On those rare occasions when a real shoe was necessary, it was inevitably accompanied by a flimsy and oh-so-dissatisfying cotton sock. Not until college, and the damp chill of San Francisco Bay Area winters (and summers), did I discover the pure joy of a well-made wool sock. By the time I turned the heel on my very own pair of handknitted socks, I was hooked. Now I have drawers, baskets, and boxes overflowing with wool socks—many handknitted, some not—yet I continue to covet them and create more. A good sock is magical.

The Knitter's Book of Socks is dedicated to all the avid sock knitters, new and old alike, whose passion and quest for knowledge were the genesis of this book. It began with a class I taught at the 2009 Sock Summit in Portland, Oregon, called "Finding Sock Yarn Happiness." As I began researching the unique yarn requirements for a good sock— and sharing this information with other sock knitters—I quickly realized that this vast amount of intriguing and yet unexplored information was begging for a book.

At Potter Craft, three bright and trusting women believed in this idea right from the start: Lauren Shakely, Victoria Craven, and Joy Aquilino. Lauren said yes, Victoria made it happen, and Joy shepherded it from my hands to yours— while my agent Linda Roghaar made sure all the gears worked smoothly and effortlessly along the way. Trust brings out the best in us, and this book is all the better because of these people's trust in me.

Cookie, Kathryn, Karen, Marlaina, Cat, Ann, Nancy, Jane, Jared, Norah, Jen, Anne, Sivia, Stephen, Melissa, Lucy, Cirilia, Sandi, and Jayme—skilled designers and friends all— understood what this book was about, willingly shared their own creative energies, and trusted me to do right by them. I thank them all. My technical editor Tamara Stone-Snyder brought the voices of these nineteen designers into perfect harmony, making sure that each word in each line of each pattern made perfect sense and was presented as intuitively as possible. She received invaluable support from Peggy Greig, whose elegant charts have graced all my books to date. I don't believe it's possible to thank these people enough, and yet I'd like to try. I also tip my hat to the many yarn companies that generously provided the yarns for the projects you see here—and I thank *all* yarn companies for continuing to put the best possible materials in our hands. We knitters can tell the difference, and we are grateful.

Speaking of knitters, a good number of the socks you see here were knit by the designers themselves. But in those cases when yarns were changed, patterns updated, and new pairs needed, I was aided by three knitting graces: Deb Barnhill, whose hands knit like the wind; Susan Sennett, whose knitting is only surpassed by her homemade toffee; and Pat Hellhake, who repeatedly managed to achieve the impossible.

At Potter Craft, Art Director Jess Morphew was faced with the daunting task of wrangling tens of thousands of my words, dozens of charts with dots and dashes and squiggly lines, and a colorful heap of knitted socks. Aided by Alexandra Grablewski and her magic camera, and Kate McKeon and her ever-charming illustrations, they brought these materials to life on the page in a beautiful, cohesive, and inspiring way. An author could not ask for a more skilled team.

To my closest friends and family, whose presence keeps me whole—to Jane, Cat, Don and Robert, Jeff and Janet, Eric and Erin, my mother and father, and the ever-lovely Beta Babes—I thank you for being patient and forgiving when the land of socks swept me up and carried me away. I thank my nieces, Hannah and Emma, and my nephews, William and Henry, for providing such perfect little feet to adorn. And I thank Clare for listening, reading, and appreciating the beauty of handknitted socks as much as I enjoy knitting them.

Index